Severe, Profound and Multiple Learning Difficulties in School

In its exploration of key debates related to curriculum, pedagogy, and policy, *Severe, Profound and Multiple Learning Difficulties in School* provokes thinking about how we reach decisions related to vulnerable learners.

The book discusses a number of 'dilemma stories' from teachers of learners with Severe, Profound, and Multiple Learning Difficulties (SPMLD). These highly evocative accounts of real situations from real classrooms serve as allegorical exemplars in relation to a range of ethical theories and prompt further dialogue and reflection. Challenging the suggestion that teaching 'some' learners is distinct from teaching 'other' learners, the central argument of this book is that the teaching of those with SPMLD should adopt a 'topographical' approach in order to be effective and ethical, seeking to look beyond the superficiality of the labels that have been applied to them. Just as a topographical cartographer or landscape artist strives to see the 'bigger picture' and represent reality, the 'topographical teacher' should seek new knowledge about their pupils and look beyond any pre-conceived labels.

This book serves to enable professionals involved in the education of those with SPMLD to engage in reflection, dialogue, and enquiry. It is an essential resource to support further study and continuing professional learning, as well as an intellectual toolkit to support developing policy and practice.

Tracy Edwards is a lecturer in Special and Inclusive Education at Leeds Beckett University, where she leads the MA Inclusive Practice in Education and PG Cert Leading SEN in International Contexts.

Severe, Profound and Multiple Learning Difficulties in School

Considering Ethical and Dilemma-Based Perspectives

Tracy Edwards

LONDON AND NEW YORK

Designed cover image: © Getty Images

First published 2026
by Routledge
4 Park Square, Milton Park, Abingdon, Oxon OX14 4RN

and by Routledge
605 Third Avenue, New York, NY 10158

Routledge is an imprint of the Taylor & Francis Group, an informa business

© 2026 Tracy Edwards

The right of Tracy Edwards to be identified as author of this work has been asserted in accordance with sections 77 and 78 of the Copyright, Designs and Patents Act 1988.

All rights reserved. No part of this book may be reprinted or reproduced or utilised in any form or by any electronic, mechanical, or other means, now known or hereafter invented, including photocopying and recording, or in any information storage or retrieval system, without permission in writing from the publishers.

Trademark notice: Product or corporate names may be trademarks or registered trademarks, and are used only for identification and explanation without intent to infringe.

British Library Cataloguing-in-Publication Data
A catalogue record for this book is available from the British Library

ISBN: 978-1-032-88877-4 (hbk)
ISBN: 978-1-032-88875-0 (pbk)
ISBN: 978-1-003-54010-6 (ebk)

DOI: 10.4324/9781003540106

Typeset in Galliard
by SPi Technologies India Pvt Ltd (Straive)

Contents

List of figures vii
List of tables viii
Preface ix
Acknowledgements xiii

Introduction 1

PART 1
Rethinking pedagogy, policy, and provision 7

1 Beyond the 'dilemma of difference' 9
2 Vulnerable learners in schools, SPMLD, and ethical theory 25
3 SPMLD, theories of learning, and debates 40

PART 2
'Dilemma Stories' from teachers of SPMLD learners 59

4 Should I be having this conversation about death? 61
5 How do we, as a team, develop an effective behavioural strategy for a learner with autism? 70
6 Is provision for Annam at our school 'good enough'? 78
7 Is it necessary to be creating art in an Art lesson? 85
8 Should pupils with PMLD be taught in age-based or needs-based provision? 91

PART 3
Developing ethical and inclusive teachers 99

9 Towards a topographical pedagogy 101

10 Dilemma-based professional learning 114

Index *135*

Figures

2.1	Nussbaum's set of 'Ten Central Capabilities'	29
9.1	A Typology of 'Four Dilemmas for Inclusive Practice'	102
9.2	Interconnections between the essences of inclusive practice with learners with SPMLD and/or at risk of exclusion	107
10.1	Process for a Lesson Study, centred around the hypothetical sensory story 'The Queen in the Garden' (adapted from the Lesson Study process outlined by Dudley, 2014)	117
10.2	Process for a 'Learning Study' for education settings with learners with SPMLD	120
10.3	A model of participation to support professional dialogues in education settings with learners with SPMLD (adapted from Treseder's 1997 'Wheel of Participation')	122
10.4	Applying the steps outlined by Tripp (2012, p.26) to the analysis of a 'critical incident,' involving a learner with SLD, in Emily's story	124
10.5	Prompts for facilitating dilemma-based dialogues between teachers	130
10.6	A process for micro dilemma-based coaching dialogues within a professional learning session	130
10.7	A card sort activity for use in a professional learning session, on dilemma-based coaching, through which participants arrange the various 'tips' for coaches	131

Tables

1.1	A Typology of Four Dilemmas for Inclusive Practice	19
9.1	An overview of 'topographical' practices in art, cartography, and education	110
10.1	Using the Engagement Model to make notes of Katie's responses to the sensory story 'The Queen in the Garden' as part of a Lesson Study	118
10.2	Using Hart's Ladder of Participation to explore the participation of learners with SPMLD in schools	122
10.3	Card sort activity to provoke discussion on the stories	128

Preface

Just as I started writing this book, I watched the stage play 'Laughing Boy' at the *Jermyn Street Theatre in London*. It is a play that tells the tragic story of Connor Sparrowhawk and his family's painful fight for justice for him. In 2013, Connor, at the age of 18, died an entirely preventable death, whilst under the care of a residential NHS facility in Oxfordshire. As well as exposing professional negligence and failures in care, the play exposes an absence of appropriate values and ethics for working with individuals with learning disabilities. In the words of Connor's mother, Sara Ryan, these individuals were being viewed as 'problems, not people.' An inspection report into the facility, which was published after Connor's death, found multiple safeguarding breaches that were seemingly indicative of a lack of concern, or respect for its residents. However, statistics cited in the play, around the premature deaths of people with learning disabilities (and the low percentage of inquests into them) suggest that this lack of concern is systematic, and by no means confined to the story of Connor, or to any single institution.

Such a lack of concern is also not confined to the health and social care sectors. In education, stories have emerged about how those with special educational needs and disabilities (SEND) have experienced the school system. At the time of writing, much has fairly recently featured in the news, about the recent history of Whitefield's Special School in East London, which was found by inspectors in 2017, to be inappropriately placing children and young people in seclusion rooms for extended periods of time, without adequate risk assessment or management (OFSTED, 2017). A later investigation of CCTV footage from padded cells that were installed at the school found that staff had been using excessive force, which had included kicking and slapping children and young people. This investigation also found that children were placed in isolation for up to four hours, sometimes eating crumbs from the floor and/or lying in their own urine (BBC, 2024).

What is significant, from my perspective, in relation to this, is that Whitefield School was otherwise seen to be highly successful. I remember, from myself working in the special school sector back in 2017, that many of its young people benefitted from fantastic vocational learning opportunities, which prepared them for paid employment. As a recognised centre of excellence, it had been awarded national 'Teaching School' status, so it had a role in the training of educators. The 2017 OFSTED report on Whitefield praises the outstanding progress that a large proportion of its pupils seemed to be making.

Similarly, based on my own experiences, I personally have no doubt that there are very many mainstream schools out there that are generally regarded as high performing and successful, yet unnecessarily exclude learners with special educational needs, under circumstances which, with ethical reasoning and dialogue in place, would be avoidable. Throughout my career, I have encountered particularly complex learning needs within education settings designated for pupils who had been excluded from multiple schools, which were only beginning to be identified. Although the overwhelming majority of such pupils are unlikely to have Severe and/or Profound and Multiple Learning Difficulties (which this particular book focusses on) their experiences, which are documented in the related research literature, reflects those same professional attitudes of seeing 'problems' rather than 'people,' which Connor Sparrowhawk's mother, Sara Ryan, describes.

Interacting with ethical and dilemma-based perspectives on professional practice, therefore, is not a mere intellectual indulgence or distraction from the 'real' business of running a school or service. It is an absolute necessity. A teacher, psychiatrist, or nurse may possess all the technical skills and knowledge to perform their role. Without regular interaction with ethics, however, professional practice will only ever be that – a 'performance', more concerned with satisfying its audience, rather than in addressing the dark realities of harm and injustice that are developing backstage.

In my experience, however, ethical professional conduct is not only about avoiding the most extreme (yet sadly, all too frequent) scenarios. It is also about ensuring that opportunities are not missed, so that individuals can benefit from them. It is about ensuring that all possible steps are being taken to enable individuals to reach the most positive outcomes obtainable, to enjoy a full and rewarding life. In the education of pupils with SPMLD, this can mean addressing questions around curriculum or having systems and processes in place to ensure that any individual learning goals that are devised for these pupils are the right ones, in relation to their points of learning and aspirations. It can also mean carefully planning school trips, or events such as summer fayres to address barriers to participation of pupils and their families, and establish the conditions for full engagement.

This book is broadly based on a series of 'dilemma stories,' from teachers of learners with an SPMLD profile, that were collected by me, as part of my PhD research. To protect the identities of the individuals within these stories, some details have been slightly changed. However, care has been taken to maintain fidelity to the teachers' own words and the situations they presented me with, as a researcher, when working with them.

Each of the stories captures a dilemma that the teacher, who kindly shared their story with me, encountered in their practice. The majority of these dilemmas have an ethical dimension and relate to broad questions around social justice in education. In some dilemmas, practitioners are navigating questions around what constitutes 'quality' in education and striving to reach an interpretation of what is happening in their classroom that has some validity. It is the situations within the stories that are assumed to be 'problems,' rather than the 'people' within them. The range and variety of the dilemmas, across the collection of stories, highlight 'problems' as an inevitable and day-to-day feature of professional practice with SPMLD learners. However, rather than frame 'problems' as inconveniences and hinderances this book instead intends to frame them as valuable learning opportunities, as well as opportunities to deepen relationships, enable personal development, and make the job of educating those with SPMLD in schools a highly rewarding one.

This book is not a practical guide to teaching learners with SPMLD, and I am not claiming, as its author, to be an expert in working with those with an SPMLD profile. With more experience in SPMLD classrooms than I have, many teachers that I have worked with over the years in schools, taught as postgraduate students, and/or interviewed as research participants, are likely to have specific insights into SPMLD classroom practice, which I lack. Rather than practical guidance, therefore, this book outlines key debates around learners with SPMLD. It has been written, for example, to support leaders within schools, local authorities, inspectorates, and/or multi-academy trusts (who may or may not have much prior experience with SPMLD learners) with their strategic thinking.

Rather than being based on a career that has been entirely focussed on teaching learners with SPMLD, this is a book that benefits from my experiences of teaching in a mainstream secondary school in East London for ten years, as well as my experiences as a school leader within a special school where there were learners with SPMLD. It also benefits from the visibility I have been privileged enough to have, as an education consultant and academic, to a wide range of classroom contexts and national school systems. My expectation is that the majority of those reading this book will be following careers in education that have taken unanticipated twists and turns, just like mine. The intention of this book, therefore, is to support education professionals to navigate these twists and turns, and any encounters with learners with SPMLD that may occur as they take them. This is the book that I wish I could have read in the summer after I left my job as a Head of Humanities in a mainstream secondary school, to start a leadership position, in that September, in an all-age specialist setting. It is also the book that I wish could have been available to me a few years later, as the specialist setting I joined expanded to include more SPMLD pupils, and I found myself leading teams in related improvement planning, and innovation around curriculum and assessment.

More than anything, however, I set about writing this book as one which I wished was available for teachers at schools such as Whitefield, and for professionals who seem to have regarded my own niece, who herself has severe learning difficulties, as a 'problem' rather than a 'person,' over the years. From my extensive background in teaching and school leadership, I became an academic and philosopher of education because I firmly believe that it is only through intellectual and ethical reasoning that we can ensure high-quality outcomes for vulnerable learners, including those with SPMLD. My intention for this book is for it to play a small role in keeping this intellectual and ethical reasoning alive, as it is something which (as the story of Connor Sparrowhawk shows us) we cannot take for granted or assume will be maintained without deliberate effort.

I hope that you find this book provocative, exciting, and stimulating, and that it supports any deliberate efforts you might be making to keep the fire of intellectual and ethical reasoning, in relation to learners with SPMLD, burning.

Tracy Edwards 19/04/25

References

BBC (2024, 26th November). *CCTV shows pupils abused and locked in padded room*. Retrieved from: https://www.bbc.co.uk/news/articles/cjw0e3zjx2lo

OFSTED. (2017). *School Report: Whitefields School*. Retrieved from: https://files.ofsted.gov.uk/v1/file/2670041

Acknowledgements

Whilst writing this book, I have benefitted enormously from being part of the department for Digital and Transformative Education within Leeds Beckett University. I would like to sincerely thank my colleagues within this team for their encouragement and support. In particular, I would like to thank Steve Burton and Meri Nasilyan, who lead this team, for their interest in my work and for their supportive conversations.

I would also like to thank Mhairi Beaton, Rachel Shanks, and Kirsten Darling-McQuistan, who supervised my PhD research at the University of Aberdeen, on which much of the discussion within this book is based. Although my PhD supervision ended some time ago, my connection with the three of them certainly hasn't!

It is through working and conversing with inspiring classroom practitioners and school leaders that my insight into severe and profound and multiple learning difficulties has developed. I am especially grateful for the conversations I have enjoyed over the years with Nathan Taylor and Becca Grant. These conversations have inspired me. They have also challenged my thinking, whilst giving me confidence in the contributions that I have to make to sector-wide dialogues on teaching vulnerable learners.

Finally, I would like to express my most sincere thanks to my friends (Thien Huong, Federica, James, Ruby, and others) whose love and support kept me going over the difficult months during which this book was being written.

Introduction

This book starts with an appreciation that learners exist across the age range, within national school systems, who are at a very low cognitive level and are unlikely to ever progress beyond early developmental milestones that tend to typically occur between birth and the age of five. These learners may have degenerative neurological conditions, severe acquired brain injuries, rare genetic traits, and/or may have been born at very early stages of gestation. Some will be working on counting to five. Others need intensive support to understand that, when an object is covered up, it is still there, or support to link cause and effect through pressing 'switches' connected to devices, to make things happen. In the context of the English school system, the vast majority of these learners will attend special schools and be identified with either 'Severe Learning Difficulties' (SLD) or 'Profound and Multiple Learning Difficulties' (PMLD). In a tiny proportion of English local authorities, and very many countries in Europe, they will attend mainstream schools, often in attached specialist units or classes such as those I have personally encountered in Sweden and Portugal. Globally, it must be acknowledged that many children and young people with such a profile will not be in education at all.

What Are Severe and Profound and Multiple Learning Difficulties?

There is no universally agreed-upon definition of 'SLD' or 'PMLD' and no accompanying criteria to support their identification. Terminology also varies between contexts. Using the language of the current Diagnostic and Statistical Manual of Mental Disorders (American Psychological Association, 2022) for example, what may be referred to as 'Severe and/or Profound and Multiple Learning Difficulties' in the English school system, is likely to instead be referred to as an 'intellectual disability' or 'intellectual development disorder' which is 'severe' or 'profound' in nature (p. 41).

A meta-analysis of different classification and assessment frameworks found that, on average, an intelligence quotient score (IQ) of 50 or lower meets the threshold for having a 'Severe Learning Difficulty' (Patel et al., 2020). According to the International Classification of Diseases and Related Health Problems (World Health Organisation, 2024), the threshold is seemingly lower, and those who have a severe or profound and multiple learning difficulty are deemed to be within the 0.003rd percentile or lower for 'intellectual functioning and adaptive behaviour' (p. 94). The English National Health Service, however, defines a person with Profound and Multiple Learning Disabilities as someone who has a Severe Learning Difficulty, alongside 'other disabilities that significantly affect their ability to communicate and be independent' (NHS, 2025). This arguably suggests vast heterogeneity within each of the two categories (of 'Severe Learning Difficulties' and 'Profound and Multiple Learning Difficulties'), as well as overlaps and intersections between them. Under the NHS definition, for example, a learner with cerebral palsy and epilepsy, who can communicate using Makaton signing, and has an IQ assessed at around 50, may be viewed as having 'Profound and Multiple Learning Difficulties', whereas a pre-verbal young person with an IQ assessed at 25, who is walking independently, and has no immediate medical needs, could be viewed as having a 'Severe Learning Difficulty.' It is certainly my experience that the use of IQ scores in labelling is highly controversial, and that labels tend to be applied in different ways, in different contexts. It is also my experience that those who share the same label of, 'SLD' or 'PMLD', can present in entirely different ways to one another.

In many education settings, it is not possible or desirable to neatly separate learners with 'SLD' and learners with 'PMLD' into different classes within a school. Learners with the label 'SLD', for example, may also have a life-limiting condition and require respiratory equipment. Others may present with distressed behaviours which are physical in nature and can pose a degree of risk to the medically vulnerable. In some schools, the number of learners with 'PMLD' may be so small that it is actually not possible to create a viable teaching group, exclusively for learners with this label. For these reasons, this book works with the umbrella term 'Severe and Profound and Multiple Learning Difficulties' (SPMLD).

The Prevalence of SPMLD

Since the mid-2000s, observations that more pupils with more complex special educational needs are entering the English school system have steered many strategic dialogues relating to special and inclusive education. Male and Rayner (cited in Male 2015, p. 11) found, for example, that a large proportion of headteachers were perceiving their schools as rapidly changing places, within which the numbers of learners with SPMLD, autism, challenging behaviour, and/or life-limiting conditions were growing. According to Carpenter et al. (2011), there have been various reasons for this, including older parents, greater numbers of infants surviving premature birth, and a higher prevalence of alcohol and substance misuse (pp. 14–15).

Between 2010 and 2018, the number of school-aged children and young people in England with PMLD increased by 1352, to 10,0032 (Public Health England, 2020), representing an increase of 16%. Between 2010 and 2020, the number of school-aged children and young people with SLD had grown by 17%. As a proportion of those in the school system, the number of pupils with SPMLD has been consistently exceptionally low, representing less than 2% of the total school population. However, the increases in actual numbers have made the development of provision for SPMLD a priority at a local and national level, making the creation of appropriate school places, and the development of related leadership capacity, imperative.

In more recent years, the number of pupils with either 'Severe Learning Difficulties' or 'Profound and Multiple Learning Difficulties' identified as their primary need may be starting to slightly plateau. The number of pupils with Education and Health Care Plans (EHCPs) with an identified primary need of 'Profound and Multiple Learning Difficulties', for example, fell from 10,003 in 2019–2020, to 9,976 the following year. The latest figure of those with PMLD in the school system, from 2023 to 2024, is 10,114. Over this time, the number of children in the English school system with autism identified as a primary need has been rising exponentially, with the total number of pupils with autism as a primary need being 100,181 in 2015–2016 and increasing to 132,249 in 2023–2024 (UK Gov, 2025). Although I have personally encountered huge inconsistencies between schools and local authorities in how SEND needs are identified, these figures suggest that trends around SEN shift, and that any specialist approaches we train teachers in today, around particular labels, may be insufficient in preparing them for the pupils they encounter tomorrow. In order to meet the needs of learners with SEN, therefore, school leaders, and teacher education, needs to be sufficiently agile.

Challenging Ableism

Emphasising the reality of having SPMLD and of the extremely low cognitive levels associated with them is, in my view, crucially important. In recent years, we have seen campaigns, for example, for teaching all children to read, irrespective of their stage in development, based on the claim that alternative specialist approaches, such as those planned with SPMLD learners in mind, deny individuals their entitlement to the same learning opportunities as non-disabled pupils. The story of Jonathan Bryan will be familiar to many teachers working in special education settings in the English context. Jonathan was a young man whose life sadly ended in June 2025, just as the edits to this book were being finalised. With his family, he was part of a campaign to ensure that no child endures the experience he lived through, of being placed in a class for learners with 'Profound and Multiple Learning Difficulties' and not being taught to write. Through the contribution he made to debates around curriculum and learners with SPMLD, Jonathan has left behind a significant legacy. Editing discussions, in several places within this book, by changing the present tense into the past tense, in relation to him, has felt incredibly poignant.

In my own experience, however, conversations about cohorts of learners with SPMLD have focussed on the possibility of there being a 'hidden genius' beneath the external appearance of a body with apparent physical limitations. Such conversations have typically involved comments such as 'when you get to know them, they may be the next Stephen Hawking.' They have also led to the use of overly complex language by classroom practitioners, as well as assumptions of intentionality behind behaviours such as throwing objects, that have actually been reflex responses and/or pre-intentional. Such conversations have also led to situations where precious curriculum time has been spent on delivering lessons on subjects such as Maths or Geography, which become staged for the purpose of demonstrating that teaching is 'ambitious.' The absurdity of this has been articulated, to powerful effect, in Penny Lacey's seminal writings on curriculum and assessment for learners with PMLD, for example, in the following cited curriculum target for 'Carl', for 'History', which does not seem purposeful and/or related to actual historical understanding:

> When presented with the 3 pictures to choose from, Carl will point to a shield, a bow and a spear correctly 3 times in the week.
> (Lacey, 2010, p. 17)

This book is based on the principle that the educability of learners with SPMLD is not contingent on them one day being able to access subjects such as Science or History, or on there being a possibility of unlocking the 'Stephen Hawking' within. It maintains that teaching and learning can be highly purposeful within a reality in which severe or profound neurological barriers to academic engagement will persist. In fact, a discourse of academic advancement and unlocking 'genius' could be viewed as symptomatic of a meritocratic society in which status and success are associated with the realisation of alleged innate ability, and fortune is celebrated as 'self-made.' The term 'ableism' refers to a form of prejudice that tends to occur within such a society, in which those deemed to have 'merit' are valued more than others. According to the American philosopher Micheal Sandel (2021), meritocratic ideas have underpinned the formation of Western democracies, and an associated 'rhetoric of rising' (p. 19), which emphasises the belief that rewards come to those who nurture their talents through hard work. Critical disability scholars have traced such rhetoric back to the European Enlightenment of the eighteenth century, which linked intellectual advancement to the emancipation of humanity from alleged savagery. This rhetoric has also been linked to colonialism, through which social groups were categorised in a way that represented the most powerful as naturally superior (e.g., Goodley, 2020). This book is based on the argument that providing appropriate schooling for those with SPMLD requires us to rethink this 'rhetoric of rising' and the meritocratic assumptions that comments such as 'they may be the next Steven Hawking' seem to be based on. According to this book, therefore, we need to reject ableism and insist that education can be purposeful with broader aims, related to strengthening the overall capacity of individuals to lead a fuller and more enriched life.

About This Book

This book is divided into three parts:

Part 1 outlines some intellectual tools for rethinking pedagogy, policy, and provision for learners with SPMLD. It presents selected ethical theories and how they might be applied to decision-making processes in school settings. It also explores debates related to the education of learners with SPMLD, such as those that relate to curriculum, assessment, and routes into the teaching profession.

Part 2 discusses selected 'dilemma stories' relating to teaching learners with SPMLD, which were collected as part of my PhD research. Ethical theories, professional values, and perspectives on curriculum, pedagogy, and assessment are applied to the discussion of each dilemma.

Part 3 outlines approaches that can be adopted within education settings that include learners with SPMLD. It presents a framework, for example, for a unique 'topographical pedagogy' through which teachers meaningfully interact with shifting realities within their classroom. It also discusses approaches to the professional learning of educators, which are 'dilemma-based' and serve to strengthen connections between classroom practice and professional values.

References

American Psychiatric Association. (2022). DSM-5-TR classification. In *Diagnostic and Statistical Manual of Mental Disorders*. Retrieved from https://doi.org/10.1176/appi.books.9780890425787.x00_diagnostic_classification

Carpenter, B., Brooks, T., Cockbill, B., Fotheringham, J., & Rawson, H. (2011). *Complex Learning Difficulties and Disabilities Research Project: Final Report*. Retrieved from https://complexneeds.org.uk/modules/Module-3.2-Engaging-in-learning---key-approaches/All/downloads/m10p010d/the_complex_learning_difficulties.pdf

Goodley, D. (2020). The psychology of disability. In N. Watson & S. Vehmas (Eds.), *Routledge Handbook of Disability Studies* (2nd ed., pp. 362–377). Routledge.

Lacey. P. (2010). SMART and SCRUFFY Targets. *The SLD Experience*, 57(1), 16–21.

Male, D. (2015). Learners with SLD and PMLD: Provision, policy and practice. In: Lacey, P., Ashdown, R., Jones, P., Lawson, H., Pipe, M. (Eds)., *The Routledge Companion to Severe, Profound and Multiple Learning Difficulties* (pp. 9–19) London: Routledge.

National Health Service. (2025, 6th May). *Learning Disabilities*. Retrieved from https://www.nhs.uk/conditions/learning-disabilities/#:~:text=A%20profound%20and%20multiple%20learning,%2C%20hearing%2C%20speaking%20and%20moving.

Patel, D. R., Cabral, M. D., Ho, A., & Merrick, J. (2020). A clinical primer on intellectual disability. *Translational Pediatrics*, 9. https://doi.org/10.21037/TP.2020.02.02

Public Health England. (2020, 27 January). *People with learning disabilities in England*. Retrieved from https://www.gov.uk/government/publications/people-with-learning-disabilities-in-england

Sandel, M. J. (2021). *The Tyranny of Merit: What's Become of the Common Good?* New York: Penguin Random House.

UK Gov. (2025, 6th May). Special Educational Needs in England. Retrieved from https://explore-education-statistics.service.gov.uk/find-statistics.special-educational-needs-in-england/2023-24

World Health Organisation. (2024). *Clinical Descriptions and Diagnostic Requirements for ICD-11 Mental, Behavioural and Neurodevelopmental Disorders*. Geneva: World Health Organisation.

Part 1

Rethinking pedagogy, policy, and provision

Chapter 1

Beyond the 'dilemma of difference'

Various principles, professional values, and theoretical ideas inevitably underpin conversations around provision, policy, and practice for learners with Special Educational Needs and Disabilities (SEND). The SEND Code of Practice for England (Department of Education and Department of Health, 2014), for example, emphasises principles such as having regard for the 'views, wishes and feelings' of the learner with SEND, involving parents, maximising participation of children and young people in decision-making processes and enabling children and young people to gain greater independence, to prepare them for adulthood' (p. 19). Although such principles may initially seem to be common-sense and uncontroversial, this chapter prompts a rethinking of them by exploring how, without dialogue and reflection, they risk being translated and enacted in ways that are not helpful to learners with SPMLD. It does this by taking the following selected principles and/or theoretical ideas in turn, and discussing the ambiguities, tensions, and debates that are inherent within each one:

- Inclusion
- Promoting independence
- Age-appropriateness
- The 'dilemma of difference'

Rethinking 'Inclusion'

One key idea where there are multiple ambiguities, debates, and tensions is that of 'inclusion' itself. In the context of education, it is a term that is exceptionally difficult to define. On one hand, there is a global movement for educational 'inclusion' and against the alleged segregation of particular children and young people, away from ordinary schools. On the other hand, in my experience, 'inclusion' has alternatively been viewed as a dogmatic ideology that is actually harmful to those who are arguably likely to be further marginalised (rather than meaningfully 'included') within a mainstream school setting.

The global movement for inclusion in education is associated with various international agencies, academic networks and non-governmental organisations. Its advocates tend to cite the seminal UNESCO Salamanca Statement of 1994 (UNESCO, 1994), which states that those 'with special educational needs must have access to regular schools ... unless there are compelling reasons for doing otherwise' (p. 4). Within this movement, 'inclusion' is linked to social justice and viewed as a moral imperative. In the foreword to the UNESCO 2020 Global Education Monitoring Report on 'Inclusion and Education' (Clark 2020, p. v) analogies are made between advocating for inclusion in education in the twenty-first century, for example, and arguing for the abolition of slavery in the nineteenth century.

However, much has been written about an apparent dissonance between the rhetoric of 'inclusion' in education and the reality of lived experiences of it of children with SEND. According to Webster (2022), for example, segregation still occurs within mainstream schools and that being physically placed somewhere within a mainstream school building, does not necessarily provide an 'inclusive' education. In their essay 'Inclusion Is Dead', Imray and Colley (2017) argue that 'inclusion' for learners with SPMLD is simply not feasible, given their requirement for entirely distinct curricula and pedagogies, from those provided to the majority. It is through such arguments that the word 'inclusion', amongst many of the SPMLD practitioners I have personally worked with, is viewed negatively, associated with naivety, and with putting ideology before actual children and young people for whom mainstream education is arguably not suited.

Just as attending a mainstream school does not guarantee a mainstream education, however, it could alternatively be argued that attending a specialist school does not by any means guarantee a positive educational experience that leads to better outcomes in life. Although the points raised by Imray and Colley are entirely valid and undoubtedly resonate with so many professionals and families, the alternatives to 'inclusion' they advocate for should also not be viewed as unambiguously positive. Simmons' study on the experiences of learners with PMLD, spending time with learners in mainstream schools (Simmons, 2021), for example, can be applied to challenge the passive and uncritical use of some of the 'separate and distinct' (Imray and Hinchcliffe, 2012, p. 150) approaches that Imray and Colley refer to. Simmons found that when children with PMLD spent time visiting a mainstream school, they were 'freed from specialist pedagogy' (p. 838), which had most likely become repetitive, uninspiring and highly technical. Although Simmons did not reach any conclusions in relation to debates around where children with PMLD should be educated, he found that more playful interactions between young people and teachers, which were not attributed to any particular specialist methodology or approach, enabled significant learning and development for individual pupils with PMLD, who were part of his study.

Across the research literature on the principle of Inclusive Pedagogy, it is argued that the same exact action within a classroom can be simultaneously inclusive and exclusive rather than unambiguously either one of the other (e.g., Black-Hawkins and Florian 2012, p. 568). In writing about this within her PhD thesis, Linklater (2010, p. 216) gives the hypothetical example of a child playing alone, in a sandpit at the corner of a classroom. On one hand, this may reflect how they are being neglected and ignored by the teacher, who is leaving them to their own devices, so that they can get on with teaching the rest of the class. On the other hand, it may reflect a positive learning environment within which children are granted the agency to get out of their seats, and draw upon the resources around them, to support learning, for example, by going over to the sandpit to support them to solve a problem relating to volume and capacity in Mathematics. When relating this argument to children and young people in schools with SPMLD, we may start to appreciate that teaching these learners may be less about promoting the wholesale use of a specific curriculum or approach, and more about developing reflective classroom practitioners who can make contextualised decisions that may vary between different individuals with the same labels or diagnoses.

With the point in mind that the same action within a classroom may be simultaneously inclusive and exclusive, it may be that the challenges and ambiguities related to 'inclusion' in education may stem from the word 'inclusion' itself. The adjective 'inclusive' has been proposed as a preferable alternative to 'inclusion' by Graham and Slee (2008). Their central argument is that, rather than embracing diversity and the uniqueness of each individual within a classroom, the notion of 'inclusion' emphasises the 'bringing in' of those who are perceived to be different from the norm, thus perpetuating a sense of 'otherness' and arguably maintaining an exclusionary status quo. From my perspective, the term 'inclusion' also carries with it a suggestion of finality and perfectionism. The term 'inclusive', however, shifts the emphasis, within professional conversations, towards the continual journey of improvement. The term 'inclusive' also seems to address complex classroom realities in which both inclusive and exclusive practices inevitably co-occur, requiring ongoing refinement and evaluation. Applying these arguments, it would be most likely more beneficial, therefore, for schools to focus on developing 'inclusive practice', rather than on delivering 'inclusion'. In relation to pupils with SPMLD, it may also mean transcending debates around mainstream and special education, and interacting with pupils' nuanced responses to classroom activities, in order to meaningfully extend their learning and participation.

We may decide, however, after giving it careful consideration, to maintain an insistence on the term 'inclusion', for example, due to the appeal of its aspirational nature, and a commitment to not compromise away from it, as an ideal. If so, the much-cited definition of 'Inclusion' as 'the processes of increasing the participation of students in, and reducing their exclusion from, the curricula, cultures and communities of local schools' (Ainscow et al., 2006,

p. 25) may be helpful. As a definition, it is potentially a helpful starting point for discussion. Is this learner participating? Do they genuinely and authentically belong? It is a definition that would be useful to a school, for example, when planning and evaluating their involvement in events such as Christmas concerts and sports days.

Many frameworks for evaluating inclusive education globally view inclusion as involving something much broader than considerations around pupils with SEND, and much has been written about the addressing of disparities, such as those around race and/or gender, as being integral to it. In the author's experience, this can support a recognition of needs that may be less immediately visible, as well as a recognition of intersectionality, which is the idea that, rather than seeing barriers that individuals face in isolation, we should engage with the multiple identities a person has and how they interact with one another (Crenshaw, 1994).

According to Florian (2012), a broader definition of inclusion, that moves away from narrow associations with SEND, is of paramount importance. Such a broad definition, she argues, makes inclusion the responsibility of all teachers, rather than something that is perceived to be the exclusive concern of specialist SEN teachers or Special Educational Needs Coordinators (SENCOs) in schools. There is an alternative argument, however, that, whilst agreeing that inclusion needs to be conceptualised as involving all learners, rather than only those learners with SEND, we also need to challenge the idea that SEND is the concern of some teachers and not others, rather than concede to it. As someone with experience of both teaching learners with SPMLD and learners with high academic attainment applying to prestigious universities, I am personally of the view that there is more that connects the two than distinguishes them. It is also noteworthy that learners with SPMLD have been found to be absent from research and policy dialogues on inclusive education. Colley (2020) argues that, although studies exist which claim to relate to the inclusion of pupils with SPMLD, it becomes evident that the learners involved were working at a far higher cognitive level for this to actually be the case. Colley's argument can be seen as a warning against marginalising SEND within debates around inclusive education. Rather than emphasising that 'inclusion' is the business of all teachers (through promoting a broader definition of it), we should arguably be emphasising, in my own opinion, that all learners, including those with SPMLD, are all teachers' collective responsibility.

In my experience, although pupils with SPMLD may be in special schools, the classes in which they learn will also be highly diverse, and an inclusive pedagogical approach to their 'special' education will be required. An individual pupil with SPMLD for example, may not have any intentional communication and be only giving reflex responses to stimuli, yet be learning alongside those that are making a range of vocalisations to indicate enjoyment, or can point to a photograph of a chosen activity (which, unlike an object, can be a too abstract representation of something for many with SPMLD). If classroom practice fails to engage with such diversity, then the education of these pupils, in my own view, can never be truly 'inclusive'. Of course, under a different, more literal definition of 'inclusion', that is associated with school placement, my view could be challenged with the argument that those with SPMLD should not be educated within mainstream schools, meaning that being 'inclusion' isn't anything that those working with these pupils should be aiming for anyway. However, if, as Ainscow et al suggest, we view 'inclusion' as being concerned with increasing participation and reducing exclusion, if we see that inclusion manifests itself in different ways in different contexts, and also recognise that, as a concept, it is multi-dimensional, then it becomes imperative to the education of SPMLD pupils in specialist settings, as well as mainstream ones.

However, whilst transcending debates around special or mainstream schools (and appreciating that exclusion and inclusion inevitably occur within any setting), we should also not ignore the possible relationship between the invisibility of learners with SPMLD within mainstream education, and the bleak life outcomes that they statistically have an increased likelihood of. In England, although statistics on such outcomes tend to be collected in relation to the broader category of 'learning disabilities', rather than in relation to SPMLD per se, they highlight an increased likelihood of those within this broader category being in poverty (British Association of Social Workers, 2023), of being victims of crime (Macdonald et al., 2023) and of being confined within their homes, unable to access public spaces and/or transport to get to them (McClimens et al., 2014). It is apparent, therefore, that within wider society, the full humanity of those with learning disabilities, including those with SPMLD, tends not to be recognised. The overwhelming evidence of their mistreatment and discrimination suggests that they can be perceived, across wider society, as an almost-subhuman 'other'. Would this still be the case if we worked, as a society, to create opportunities for children and young people with SPMLD to play and learn together?

In her writings about education, the Indian postcolonial theorist Spivak (1988) emphasises the value of the 'ethical engagement with the other' through which interaction is facilitated between those with different labels, and misperceptions and stereotypes are 'unlearned' (cited in Andreotti, 2007, p. 70). According to Spivak's arguments, without investment in this 'ethical engagement with the other', binary distinctions around difference become assumed, such as rich/poor, black/white, disabled/non-disabled. These binary distinctions ultimately serve to dehumanise those who are already marginalised, thus reproducing historic inequalities and patterns of oppression. Although such arguments are difficult to apply to day-to-day decision-making within schools where learners with SPMLD are educated, they serve to highlight how the injustices they are ultimately at serious risk of are not due to the isolated actions of rogue individuals. Instead, they are rooted in patterns of thinking, shaped by historical forces, that have become systemic and need to be disrupted.

Rethinking 'Promoting Independence'

Another value that has been found to be central to inclusive practice in education is that of 'promoting independence'. The origins of this value can be traced back to the Independent Living Movement, which emerged in the United Kingdom in the late 1970s, taking inspiration from the rising tide of disability activism in the United States of America. The Independent Living Movement rejected the inherent paternalism in dominant approaches to disability, which disability activists were encountering at the time, such as the medicalised approaches which were based on the idea that physical differences were problems to be 'fixed' rather than a dimension to human diversity and variation. The Independent Living Movement also challenged the prevailing assumption, which disability activists were also encountering in the 1970s, that a person's capacity to make decisions was contingent on them having a 'normal' body. The principle of 'promoting independence', therefore, shaped the philosophical foundations of a global movement that effectively campaigned for civil rights. The history of this movement is so inspirational, and the impact it has made on national, local, and organisational policies has been highly significant, undoubtedly making a positive difference to so many lives. The protests that took place through this movement also gave visibility to the creativity, talent, and sexuality of disability activists, thus challenging perceptions of disabled people as pathetic, sick, asexual and dependent on others. The movement also promoted the Social Model of Disability (Shakespeare and Watson, 1997; Durell, 2014), which emphasises how it is wider society, with its negative attitudes and failures to make adjustments, that makes a person 'disabled', rather than any perceived defects.

The principle of 'promoting independence', therefore, has had such an important role to play in improving lives, and the suggestion that we rethink it, in the context of pupils with SPMLD, feels controversial and dangerous. However, my own view is that, whilst focussing on maximising the self-determination of PMLD pupils, for example, we also need to work with the reality of their levels of communication and cognition and the chronic and medical nature of their needs. We must also recognise the role that a civilised society must play in caring for them and their dependency on others. At times, this may mean calling out an emphasis on 'promoting independence' on occasions where it may be harmful or tokenistic.

In her analysis of the 2014 SEND Code of Practice for England and Wales, Burch (2018) links the value of 'independence', which recurs throughout it, with an ideological drive to reduce the role of the welfare state and levels of state report. She highlights a stated aim within the code to 'reduce lifetime support costs to the public purse' (Department for Education and Department for Health, 2014, p. 123) of individuals with SEND, making links with the austerity policies of the Coalition government, which were responsible for its implementation. The emphasis on 'independence' within the Code of Practice,

Burch argues, reflects a political context within which many disabled people have been denied financial support to which they are entitled, to the detriment of their health and wellbeing. Citing Goodley (2014), she also argues that, due to the dominance of neoliberalism in education, the success of schools is measured in relation to the extent to which they effectively produce neo-liberal citizens, who tend not to rely on the state, and instead contribute to the economy. It is difficult, from my own perspective, for schools with a large proportion of SPMLD pupils to effectively perform such a role.

Although employment is such a positive outcome of education for so many young people with SEND, and there is an argument that we need to be aspirational for all learners, there are SPMLD learners in schools whose lives are exceptionally fragile, and for whom the Social Model of Disability can never arguably provide a full explanation or perspective on their disabilities. In the same way as an elderly person with advanced dementia requires round-the-clock care rather than employment, this is also the case for many pupils in schools with SPMLD (although by no means all of them). This requires us to rethink the purpose of education for these pupils and how we assess and evaluate success accordingly. It also requires us to reconsider the principle of 'promoting independence' and ask ourselves whether or not it applies in all situations.

In my own experience, an emphasis on 'promoting independence' can have a negative psychological and emotional impact. One young woman that I attended meetings for, for example, became so preoccupied with concerns about finances and money once she turned 18, which led to her continually directing related questions to the adults around her and engaging in distressed behaviours, such as hoarding food. This young woman struggled to understand that she was not about to be left defenceless and forced to fend for herself, yet she also seemed to have some awareness of her dependency on others. Being asked, at meeting after meeting, about her career aspirations, had evidently had a detrimental effect on her, highlighting how an alternative focus on care and protection was imperative.

Rather than the promotion of independence, Colley, Tilbury, and Yates (2021) draw upon the writings of the American philosopher Martha Nussbaum and argue that we need to focus instead on building reciprocal interdependences between learners with SPMLD and the significant others that feature in their lives. From my perspective, this has further implications for what we consider to be inclusive and exclusive practice in education. Rather than being 'inclusive', for example, there is an argument that lessons on independent living skills will only be highly tokenistic for some pupils. One example of this may be a lesson claiming to teach an individual with PMLD how to use a microwave, ending up being nothing more than the taking of staged photos of them sitting in their wheelchair next to one. Whereas it could be claimed that these photos capture steps being taken to promote the independence of this individual, the reality is likely to be that they were passive throughout them being taken, with it only being the adults around them who were active. Is that the promotion of independence, therefore, or the undermining of it?

As well as encountering an apparent difference between appearance and reality, in relation to the principle of 'promoting independence', I have also encountered a dangerous fine line between professional efforts to maximise the autonomy and agency of young people with SPMLD, and a failure of professionals to offer the required support for this to actually happen. The principle of 'promoting independence', for example, could form part of an elaborate rationale for not having resources in place, such as behaviour charts, visual timetables or 'social stories' (Gray, 1994). According to this rationale, the absence of such resources is a good thing, which provides higher levels of challenge to pupils and ultimately extends their learning. Whereas this may very well be the case for many, we have to be simultaneously mindful of how this rhetoric around 'promoting independence' can be used to justify professional inaction, neglect even. Ironically, this inaction and an associated failure to put strategies in place for learners can make them more dependent on teachers and support staff, rather than less. Rather than uncritically equating the withdrawal of support for pupils, therefore, with the promotion of independence, we need to ask the question 'What can we do to enhance this person's agency and autonomy?' For some pupils this may involve adopting approaches such as the use of 'Objects of Reference' (Park, 1995) to connect them to key events and transitions that happen during the school day. For others, it may mean implementing a Picture Exchange Communication System (PECS) to enable an individual to independently communicate wants and needs (Bondy and Frost, 1994). With many individuals, however, implementing these things would indeed be stifling and prevent them from developing the verbal expression that they have been starting to use without them. In the same way as it is argued that the exact same action in a classroom can be simultaneously inclusive and exclusive, depending on the context, it is also the case, in my experience, that the same action within a classroom can simultaneously promote independence and restrict it. This requires us to rethink the notion of 'promoting independence' and recognise that what is done in its name may not be necessarily in the individual's best interest.

Rethinking 'Age-Appropriateness'

The term 'age-appropriateness' refers to the idea that we should engage learners in ways that are deemed suitable for their chronological age, to avoid infantilising them. On a superficial level, it appears to be an entirely positive principle for schools to take on board, serving as a reminder to respect the full humanity of adolescent pupils, who may have emerging sexualities and lived experience of puberty. Just as distinctions have been made between biological sex and gender identity, it is surely also possible to distinguish between the chronological age of a person and their overall personality, which reflects their developmental level and any interests or hobbies they may have in relation to it.

Quite often, within special schools, I come across the phrase 'stage not age', referring to the idea that curriculum and assessment should address a pupil's actual point of development, rather than how old they happen to be. This idea of 'stage not age' can easily be contrasted with the notion of 'age-appropriateness'. Beyond this, however, it is my own view that teachers and schools need to balance these two ideas through a recognition that, in different situations and contexts, they may each play a role. The important thing with this is not to insist on either one or the other uncritically, but to use them merely as broad guiding principles that support difficult decision-making around individual young people.

The notion of 'age-appropriateness' has been a core value for the teaching of teenagers with SEND (Forster, 2010). One recognised challenge for teachers of secondary-aged pupils with significant reading difficulties, therefore, has been to find and/or create resources which are 'age-appropriate' whilst meeting individuals at their point of learning (McCray et al. 2001; Shurr and Kromer, 2018). Although important work has gone into developing 'age-appropriate' reading materials that reflect the literacy levels of adolescents, with low levels of literacy, an emphasis on 'age-appropriateness' could in fact be viewed as a tool of exclusion, rather than inclusion, in relation to pupils with SPMLD. This is explored by Forster (2010), who traces the notion of 'age-appropriateness' to the Social Role Valorisation Theory of Wolfenberger (1984, cited in Forster, 2010), which maintained that gaining status within society required being portrayed in ways that society valued. Forster points out that the concept of 'age-appropriateness' can, in fact, be harmful to individuals with PMLD. It represents an attempt at normalisation, and enforcing socially acceptable identities, whilst denying those that are unlikely to fit into stereotypical age-related social roles. As pointed out by Lacey (2006, cited in Forster 2010, p.130), any insistence on 'age-appropriateness' for individuals with PMLD can also represent a denial of human rights, by depriving them of stimuli (such as songs or dolls) that support their development and wellbeing.

In relation to learners with SPMLD, therefore, the principle of 'age-appropriateness' can be charged with restricting opportunities for individuals to shape new identities. Beyond SPMLD, it is a principle that arguably belongs to the twentieth century, and to a time when there were also more rigid gender and occupational roles in wider society. What can it possibly mean to be 'age-appropriate', we could ask, amongst a generation of young people that is positively challenging gender binaries? What can it possibly mean to be age-appropriate within inclusive and diverse communities in which teenagers without SPMLD are at liberty to wear a 'Hello Kitty' backpack, or watch 'Kung Fu' Panda at the cinema, if they want to?

Rethinking 'The Dilemma of Difference'

Norwich (2008, 2010, 2019) explains the 'dilemma of difference' as the conflict between a desire to identify and address individual needs of learners with

SEND in schools and wanting to simultaneously protect them from any stigma that may come with marking them out as different. Norwich points out that, in the English policy context, a 'dilemma of difference' is articulated within the seminal 1981 Warnock Report on 'The Education of Handicapped Children and Young People'. He also points out that considerations around the 'dilemma of difference' established the 'basic design of individual identification and assessment system of additional needs' and remains 'the cornerstone of the system' to the present day (Norwich 2019, p. 2).

The 'dilemma of difference' is a dilemma that, arguably, many adults would empathise with, possibly when recalling their own childhood and/or imagining the feeling of being asked to sit at a particular table in their classroom, and set a different activity to do, from that set for the majority. My own research, however, found that experienced teachers with a commitment to inclusive practice, in the twenty-first century, over 40 years since the publication of the Warnock Report, tend to conceptualise their dilemmas in alternative ways (Edwards, 2025).

The research involved the analysis of 42 'dilemma stories' from 19 experienced teachers, who needed to be in the profession for a minimum of 5 years, in order to participate. The majority of the stories (35) were crafted as part of a methodological approach which involved story-sharing dialogues with the teachers, transcription, and the (re)drafting of narratives. Each story was given a title, which represented the dilemma within it, such as 'If they are making beans and toast with us are they learning?', 'Should I be having this conversation about death?' and 'How do we manage Samiya's public, sexualised behaviours?' Out of the 42 stories analysed for the study, 24 related to the teaching of learners with SPMLD. A sample of these 24 stories is discussed in detail in Part 2 of this book. All 42 stories were analysed in relation to the research question 'What dilemmas relating to the teaching of pupils in complex and diverse classes are articulated by experienced teachers with an interest in inclusive pedagogical practice?'. The 24 stories that related to SPMLD contexts were also analysed in relation to the research question 'What is inclusive practice with learners with Severe and/or Profound and Multiple Learning Difficulties?'.

The analysis utilised the approach of phenomenography, which is the study of the variation of conceptions which are held in relation to a phenomenon (Marton, 1981). It also utilised the approaches outlined van Manen (2016) in his 'Phenomenology of Practice'. Phenomenological research is concerned with articulating lived experience(s) of the phenomenon under investigation, which, for the purposes of this study, was 'inclusive practice with students with SPMLD'. Van Manen's approaches are underpinned by processes for interpretation and reflection. The stories were therefore discussed at conferences, to enable interaction with multiple perspectives on them.

Rather than 'dilemmas of difference', the analysis found four alternative types of dilemma within the 'dilemma stories'. These have been captured in

Table 1.1 A typology of four dilemmas for inclusive practice

Dilemma	Questions this dilemma might involve
Dilemma of Possibility	Should I take a risk and try something new, which may benefit pupils? Or should I play it safe and continue with habitual practices that are deemed effective, even though they seem far from ideal?
Dilemma of 'What's Working?'	Shall we carry on with this strategy or intervention or discontinue it?
Dilemma of 'Looking'	What are these behaviours suggesting to us? Which interpretation of what we are 'seeing' should we be working with: y or z?
Dilemma of 'What Matter's?'	When we talk about 'participation' (or any other concept or value) should we take it to mean *a* or *b*? Is *x* or *y* of more value to our pupils? Which one, of the two, should we prioritise through our teaching?

a typology of 'Four Dilemmas for Inclusive Practice', which are outlined in Table 1.1, and also explained in full, below.

The Dilemma of 'Possibly'

This is a dilemma through which a teacher asks themselves about what is 'possible' or feasible in particular circumstances, or conditions. When going through this dilemma, a teacher may wonder whether or not they are being naïve when considering something that they suspect may be too ambitious. They may find themselves needing to choose between taking a risk (and changing approaches that may be suboptimal) and not disrupting established practices, which may be playing an important role in providing routine and security.

An example of a 'dilemma of possibility' can be found in the story 'Should I be having this conversation about death?'. In this story, 'Polly', a teacher within a mainstream school, finds herself grappling with internal questions about her capacity to support a pupil with SLD, 'Hafsa', who does not seem to have any awareness of the reality that life inevitably comes to an end. When teaching a Religious Education unit on 'Death and Dying', to a mixed attainment class which includes Hafsa, Polly finds herself wondering whether it is 'possible' for her to address this pupil's apparent confusion over the recent loss of her Grandad. She asks herself if it would be more appropriate for her to focus Hafsa on completing a task, such as a wordsearch or colouring sheet, to enable her lesson to run smoothly and avoid creating an emotionally charged situation, which she may not have the skills to manage. In the end, however, she concludes that she should indeed be having the conversation with this pupil about death, and that it is her moral duty, as a teacher, to work to expand the boundaries of what is 'possible'.

The Dilemma of 'What's Working?'

When navigating this dilemma, teachers are evaluating the effectiveness of strategies for supporting pupil learning to inform their continued planning. They are asking themselves, 'What's Working?'. This is something which becomes a dilemma due to competing priorities and differing views on the educational outcomes being aimed for. A strategy, which may be effective in ensuring that a learner with autism and SLD, sits through a school assembly without shouting or running out of the hall, may, on a superficial level, appear to be 'working'. However, this may not in fact be the case if this correlates with them instead expending their anxieties during the breaktime, which happens immediately following the assembly, in ways that are potentially harmful to others. Navigating this 'Dilemma of What's Working?', therefore, requires interaction with questions around what 'working' means, and recognition that what may appear to be 'working' from one perspective may not necessarily be working from another.

By asking questions around 'What's working?', we are therefore arguably moving beyond more abstract considerations of 'What works?' in education. In dominant discourses on evidence-informed pedagogy, the term "What works?" tends to be used to refer to classroom strategies that have been tested through Randomised Control Trials (RCTs), so deemed to be effective and scalable. In England, for example, the term 'What Works?' underpins the work of the Education Endowment Foundation (2021). Rather than the passive implementation of what the wider evidence dictates, navigating dilemmas around 'what's working?' involves continual assessment, reflection, and professional judgement. Whereas the term 'what works' arguably carries with it the same sense of finality and absolutism that has been associated with the term 'inclusion', the alternative term 'what's working?' is based on an appreciation that the success of any strategy is provisional. Something that may be 'working' in a particular classroom, or at a particular moment, may not necessarily always 'work' in all places, and at all times.

An example of this 'Dilemma of What's Working?' can be found in the story 'How do we, as a team, develop effective, personalised strategies for a pupil with autism?' in which 'Carlos', a Lead Practitioner within a special school, is grappling to establish 'what's working' for an individual young person presenting with challenging behaviours. For Carlos and his colleagues in this story, establishing educational effectiveness is highly situated. Rather than implement strategies that have been deemed to 'work' in the past, they are actively engaging in collaborative problem-solving to establish 'what's working' for their particular pupil at a particular point in his schooling. In doing this they are often guided by evidence-based notions of best practice and 'what works', with the use of a visual timetable, for example, being an evidence-based strategy associated with effective autism provision (Dettmer et al., 2000; Morrison et al., 2002; Pierce et al., 2013). However, the practitioners in this story have the agency to adapt and refine approaches and give their own definition to 'what's working' within their context.

Dilemmas of 'Looking'?

This dilemma involves teachers making sense of what they 'see' within their classroom, or what they encounter using other senses, such as hearing. An appreciation of this dilemma is based on a recognition that any teacher's perspective is partial, and that what can be seen in the classroom is part of a 'bigger picture' which is unlikely to ever become fully visible. It is also based on a recognition that what can be 'seen' in the classroom is inherently ambiguous. A learner, for example, may be making seemingly inappropriate animal noises during a story-telling session for a number of reasons, making it unclear to the teacher whether or not they are 'seeing' (or hearing!) intentional non-compliance, confusion, a desire to engage peers, a genuine attempt to participate (and/or a combination of several of these things!). Rather than presume what may feel obvious, engaging in dilemmas of 'looking' involves an openness to interpreting pupil behaviours in new ways, which may be more constructive than the conclusions we reach as teachers, when we may initially feel stressed, or preoccupied with the extent to which we have control. With this dilemma, classroom practitioners are often faced with a choice between continuing with practices that appear to be effective on the surface (and may be pleasing to various colleagues, senior leaders, parents, and/or inspectors) or refusing to ignore the dissonance between superficial appearance and reality, and change things.

One example of a dilemma of 'looking' is in the story 'Is provision for Annam within my tutor group good enough?' in which 'Polly', a teacher in a mainstream secondary school, was asking herself what she was 'seeing' in relation to 'Annam', a teenage pupil with SPMLD who she occasionally thought would be better placed in a secondary specialist education setting. When Polly observed the teenagers in her class interact with 'Annam', she wondered if she was 'seeing' her being infantilised by them. However, over time, she observed a genuine reciprocity between Annam and her peers, and the formation of positive relationships, which supported this pupil's development.

The 'Dilemma of What Matters?'

Intrinsically linked to the 'Dilemma of What's Working?' and to the dilemmas of 'Looking', the 'Dilemma of What Matters?' involves teachers addressing broad questions, such as those related to defining core professional values, establishing moral purpose, and/or evaluating the rationale behind school policies and practices. An example of this dilemma is in the story 'How can I support Jane to feel positive about teaching a class of learners with Profound and Multiple Learning Difficulties?' in which 'Helen', a deputy head in a special school, finds that it was moving towards engagement-based assessment processes, which enable authentic interaction with pupils' points of learning, that ultimately excites a teacher who had started to lose motivation. It was a move that empowered the teacher to engage in the 'Dilemma of What Matters?', consider the ultimate goals for her pupils, and develop a positive sense of moral purpose as a result.

The 'Dilemma of What Matters?' arguably has greater transformative potential, in relation to teaching learners with SPMLD, than the 'dilemma of difference' which has long dominated discussions since the publication of the Warnock Report. Through an analysis of the stories involving SPMLD pupils, it was evident that, when teachers interact with this 'Dilemma of What Matters?', to ultimately challenge conventions and assumed ways of 'doing things' in education, 'difference' becomes far less a 'dilemma'. It is through the 'Dilemma of What Matters?', for example, that teachers might start to question whether or not the principle of 'age-appropriateness' actually 'matters' in relation to teaching a teenager with SPMLD, who only appears responsive to the same songs from Disney Films that they have enjoyed listening to, since being a young child. It is through the 'Dilemma of What Matters?' that those teaching pupils with SPMLD can start to challenge established orthodoxies in education, rather than passively apply them in ways which may not be appropriate.

In the same way as a call to reject 'age-appropriateness' is a call to reject inherited notions of normality, moving beyond the 'dilemma of difference' is a call for us to stop benchmarking people against historic notions of typicality. Rejecting the principle of 'age-appropriateness' and thinking beyond the 'dilemma of difference' is the basis for truly inclusive school cultures which emphasise and celebrate the uniqueness of each individual. Within such cultures, teachers and schools are unlikely to be preoccupied with the 'dilemma of difference'. They are likely not to feel compelled in any way to hide or deny individual differences, or to strive to ensure that all learners conform to a perceived norm. Instead, they can meet individual needs in individualised ways without being stigmatising. They can make the difference transparent and foster an appreciation of it, as an inevitable and valuable feature of any classroom.

References

Andreotti, V. (2007). An ethical engagement with the other: Spivak's ideas on education. *Critical Literacy: Theories and Practices, 1,* 69–88.

Ainscow, M., Booth, T., Dyson, A., Farrell, P., Frankham, J., Gallannaugh, F., Howes, A., & Smith, R. (2006). *Improving schools, developing inclusion.* Retrieved from https://doi.org/10.4324/9780203967157

Black-Hawkins, K., & Florian, L. (2012). Classroom teachers craft knowledge of their inclusive practice. *Teachers and Teaching: Theory and Practice, 18*(5). https://doi.org/10.1080/13540602.2012.709732

Bondy, A. S., & Frost, L. A. (1994). The picture exchange communication system. *Focus on Autism and Other Developmental Disabilities, 9*(3). https://doi.org/10.1177/108835769400900301

Booth, T., & Ainscow, M. (2002). Index for inclusion developing learning and participation in schools: Editing and production for CSIE Mark Vaughan. *Restoration Ecology, 15*(2002).

British Association for Social Work. (2023, February 22). *Spotlight on Poverty: People with Learning Disabilities.* Retrieved from https://Basw.Co.Uk/Articles/Spotlight-Poverty-People-Learning-Disabilities

Burch, L. F. (2018). Governmentality of adulthood: A critical discourse analysis of the 2014 Special Educational Needs and Disability Code of Practice. *Disability and Society, 33*(1). https://doi.org/10.1080/09687599.2017.1383231

Butler, J. (2011). *Gender Trouble: Feminism and the Subversion of Identity*. New York and London: Routledge.

Clark, H. (2020). *Foreword to Global Education Monitoring Report; Inclusion and Education: All Means All*. Paris: UNESCO

Colley, A. (2020). To what extent have learners with severe, profound and multiple learning difficulties been excluded from the policy and practice of inclusive education? *International Journal of Inclusive Education*, 24(7). https://doi.org/10.1080/13603116.2018.1483437

Colley, A., Tilbury, J., & Yates, S. (2021). *Enhancing Wellbeing and Independence for Young People with Profound and Multiple Learning Difficulties: Lives Lived Well*. London: Routledge.

Crenshaw, K. W. (1994). Mapping the margins: Intersectionality, identity politics, and violence against women of color. In M. Albertson Fineman (Ed.), *The Public Nature of Private Violence: Women and the Discovery of Domestic Abuse*. (pp. 93–121). Routledge.

Department of Education and Department of Health. (2014). *The SEND Code of Practice*. https://www.legislation.gov.uk/ukpga/1981/60/enacted

Dettmer, S., Simpson, R. L., Myles, B. S., & Ganz, J. B. (2000). The Use of Visual Supports to Facilitate Transitions of Students with Autism. *Focus on Autism and Other Developmental Disabilities*, 15(3). https://doi.org/10.1177/108835760001500307

Durell, S. (2014). How the social model of disability evolved. *Nursing Times*, 110(50).

Education Endowment Foundation. (2021, 27th November). *EEF Launches update teaching and learning toolkit*. Retrieved from: https://educationendowmentfoundation.org.uk/about-us

Edwards, T. (2025). Beyond the 'dilemma of difference': An analysis of stories from experienced teachers, about their inclusive practice. *British Educational Research Journal*. https://doi.org/10.1002/berj.4129

Florian, L. (2012). Preparing teachers to work in inclusive classrooms: Key lessons for the professional development of teacher educators from scotland's inclusive practice project. *Journal of Teacher Education*, 63(4). https://doi.org/10.1177/0022487112447112

Forster, S. (2010). Age-appropriateness: Enabler or barrier to a good life for people with profound intellectual and multiple disabilities? *Journal of Intellectual and Developmental Disability*, 35(2). https://doi.org/10.3109/13668251003694606

Goodall, C. (2018). 'I felt closed in and like I couldn't breathe': A qualitative study exploring the mainstream educational experiences of autistic young people. *Autism and Developmental Language Impairments*, 3. https://doi.org/10.1177/2396941518804407

Goodley (2014) is cited in Burch (2018) so the intext reference should be changed from Goodley (2014) to (Goodley, 2014, cited in Burch, 2018, p. 97).

Graham, L. J., & Slee, R. (2008). An illusory interiority: Interrogating the discourse/s of inclusion. *Educational Philosophy and Theory*, 40(2). https://doi.org/10.1111/j.1469-5812.2007.00331.x

Gray, C. (1994). *The New Social Story Book*. Arlington, TX: Future Horizons.

Imray, P., & Hinchcliffe, V. (2012). Not fit for purpose: A call for separate and distinct pedagogies as part of a national framework for those with severe and profound learning difficulties. *Support for Learning*, 27(4). https://doi.org/10.1111/1467-9604.12002

Imray, P., & Colley, A. (2017). Inclusion is dead: Long live inclusion. In *Inclusion is Dead: Long Live Inclusion*. https://doi.org/10.4324/9781315280059

Linklater, H. (2010). *Making children count?: An autoethnographic exploration of pedagogy*. Thesis (PhD). University of Aberdeen.

Macdonald, S. J., Donovan, C., & Clayton, J. (2023). 'I may be left with no choice but to end my torment': Disability and intersectionalities of hate crime. *Disability and Society*, 38(1). https://doi.org/10.1080/09687599.2021.1928480

van Manen, M. (2016). Phenomenology of practice. *Phenomenology of Practice*. https://doi.org/10.4324/9781315422657

Marton, F. (1981). Phenomenography - Describing conceptions of the world around us. *Instructional Science, 10*(2). https://doi.org/10.1007/BF00132516

McClimens, A., Partridge, N., & Sexton, E. (2014). How do people with learning disability experience the city centre? A Sheffield case study. *Health and Place, 28.* https://doi.org/10.1016/j.healthplace.2014.02.014

McCray, A. D., Vaughn, S., & Neal, L. V. I. (2001). Not all students learn to read by third grade: Middle school students speak out about their reading disabilities. *Journal of Special Education, 35*(1). https://doi.org/10.1177/002246690103500103

Morrison, R. S., Sainato, D. M., Benchaaban, D., & Endo, S. (2002). Increasing play skills of children with autism using activity schedules and correspondence training. *Journal of Early Intervention, 25*(1). https://doi.org/10.1177/105381510202500106

Norwich, B. (2008). Dilemmas of difference, inclusion and disability: International perspectives on placement. *European Journal of Special Needs Education, 23*(4). https://doi.org/10.1080/08856250802387166

Norwich, B. (2010). Dilemmas of difference, curriculum and disability: International perspectives. *Comparative Education, 46*(2). https://doi.org/10.1080/03050061003775330

Norwich, B. (2019). From the Warnock Report (1978) to an education framework commission: A novel contemporary approach to educational policy making for pupils with special educational needs/disabilities. *Frontiers in Education, 4.* https://doi.org/10.3389/feduc.2019.00072

Park, K. (1995). Using objects of reference: A review of the literature. *European Journal of Special Needs Education, 10*(1). https://doi.org/10.1080/0885625950100104

Pierce, J. M., Spriggs, A. D., Gast, D. L., & Luscre, D. (2013). Effects of visual activity schedules on independent classroom transitions for students with autism. *International Journal of Disability, Development and Education, 60*(3). https://doi.org/10.1080/1034912X.2013.812191

Shakespeare, T., & Watson, N. (1997). Defending the social model. *Disability and Society, 12*(2). https://doi.org/10.1080/09687599727380

Shurr, J., & Kromer, G. (2018). Picture plus discussion with partners: Peer centered literacy supports for students with significant disabilities. *International Journal of Developmental Disabilities, 64*(4–5). https://doi.org/10.1080/20473869.2017.1312060

Simmons, B. (2021). The production of social spaces for children with profound and multiple learning difficulties: A Lefebvrian analysis. *British Journal of Sociology of Education, 42*(5–6). https://doi.org/10.1080/01425692.2021.1922269

Spivak, G. C. (1988). Can the Subaltern Speak?. In C. Nelson & L. Grossberg (Eds.), *Marxism and the Interpretation of Culture* (pp. 271–313). University of Illinois Press.

Sproston, K., Sedgewick, F., & Crane, L. (2017). Autistic girls and school exclusion: Perspectives of students and their parents. *Autism and Developmental Language Impairments, 2.* https://doi.org/10.1177/2396941517706172

UNESCO. (1994). *The Salamanca Statement and Framework for Action on Special Needs Education*. United Nations Educational, Scientific and Cultural Organization. https://unesdoc.unesco.org/ark:/48223/pf0000098427

Webster, R. (2022). The Inclusion Illusion: How children with special educational needs experience mainstream schools. In *The Inclusion Illusion: How Children with Special Educational Needs Experience Mainstream Schools.* https://doi.org/10.14324/111.9781787357099

Chapter 2

Vulnerable learners in schools, SPMLD, and ethical theory

Various ethical theories offer valuable intellectual tools to support decision-making around learners with SPMLD. This chapter will give an overview of these theories to introduce arguments that may strengthen professional dialogues in education settings.

Utilitarianism

The widely cited argument that teachers and schools should focus first on the best interests of the majority of the class, rather than on the individual learner whose needs are deemed to conflict with these interests, will most likely be familiar to any education professional reading this chapter. It features in debates around school exclusions, for example, which have emphasised a school's moral duty to 'the other 29' pupils in a class, whose right to an education is apparently disrupted by the behaviour of a single pupil. Similarly, in the 'special schools' debate around whether-or-not learners with SPMLD could viably be educated in mainstream school settings, questions around the feasibility of a teacher dividing their attention between an individual with complex needs and the majority of a class are, in my experience, often raised.

The assertion that decision-making, in education, needs to start with consideration for the majority of pupils has a basis in 'utilitarian' ethical theory, which is historically associated with the writings of Jeremy Bentham (1748–1832) and John Stuart Mill (1806–1873). According to utilitarianism, our actions should be informed by an appreciation of what would lead to the greatest good for the greatest number of people. It therefore presents itself as a rational approach to formulating effective policies, for example, in health care, education, and/or local government. Beyond subjective opinions around what may be the morally 'right' thing to do, a utilitarian ethicist may argue that it is more purposeful to assess the likely outcome of any choices we make, to reach decisions that will have the most tangible and positive impact on the maximum number of lives.

Learners with SPMLD, however, are a minority within school systems globally. In England, those with SLD or PMLD as their identified primary need make up less than 2% of pupils enrolled in schools (UK Gov, 2025). Classes within special schools that serve these learners can also be exceptionally diverse, with additional levels of staff and equipment inevitably being required to meet the unique needs of individuals at various times within a school day. It is difficult to apply utilitarian arguments to this reality. In fact, to do so could ultimately strengthen any unsavoury claims that children and young people with SPMLD are ineducable. Schooling these children and young people is unlikely to lead, it has historically been asserted, to them becoming economically productive, to the benefit of wider society, making the cost of it (so the argument goes) a burden to the majority of citizens.

Although these arguments may often feel confined to the past, they are evidently still going strong. In my own experience, for example, similar arguments can underpin the withdrawal of funding for school places, from English local authorities, for young people with SPMLD, at the age of 16, and associated recommendations that Education, Health and Care Plans (which tend to have cost implications) are ended. As noted by van Toorn et al. (2024), similar arguments also underpin the Australian immigration system, within which decisions are reached on the basis of an individual's capacity to contribute to the national economy. In July 2024, it was reported by the BBC that the family of two-and-a-half-year-old Luca was denied the right to remain in Australia permanently, on the grounds that the financial costs of his healthcare, for his cystic fibrosis, were too onerous and detrimental to the nation as a whole. In the same article, the case of nine-year-old Darcy, who has Down Syndrome, was also reported. Darcy's parents had been advised by immigration experts in Australia that the chances of her being granted a visa to stay in the country permanently were minimal. This is mostly due to a maximum of 170,000 Australian dollars being set by the government, as the amount an individual immigrant can cost the state over a period of 10 years. The cost of education is included in these calculations (Watson, 2024). As well as Darcy, this utilitarian logic will inevitably also impact decisions about immigration, in contemporary Australia, for those with SPMLD.

By being centred around the principle of 'the greatest good for the greatest number,' utilitarianism is an example of consequentialist ethics. It proposes that decisions are made on the basis of the anticipated result or outcome of an action. Its perspective on ethics is also what we might refer to as 'teleological.' The term 'teleological' derives from the word 'telos,' meaning 'goal.' It is a term that is associated with the writings of Aristotle and his philosophy that everything in existence is striving to fulfil its ultimate purpose. Consequentialist ethics can be challenged by pointing out that we often make decisions without actually knowing what the outcome of them will be. Consequentialist ethics can also be charged with being overly simplistic. Rather than attribute a situation or outcome to a particular single action, we should, it could be argued, instead appreciate the complex array of factors that continue to shape and reshape reality. When leading education provision for learners with SPMLD, for example, how would we eventually establish whether-or-not we are allocating different classes to the sensory room fairly? How can we assess whether-or-not the working hours of the Music teacher are being distributed in a just and appropriate way when timetabling? On what basis could we predict that a part-time support worker would be the best use of additional funding for deprived families, that would lead to the best outcomes?

Of course, teachers, school leaders, and policymakers can have access to empirical research, which enables any assessments of what should lead to the greatest good, so that their decisions are informed by robust evidence, rather than mere guesswork. In England, the Education Endowment Foundation (2025) publishes toolkits which are largely based on the results of randomised control trials of classroom interventions such as numeracy programmes or enrichment clubs. Such toolkits, it can easily be claimed, enable utilitarian calculations of the likely benefits of an action, that inform better decision-making than that which is made on the basis of 'hunches.'

However, before embracing utilitarianism as a framework for ethical school policy making and decision-making in education, it may be helpful to ask ourselves if the outcomes of the choices we make have boundaries, and if so, what these boundaries are. An initiative or strategy for teaching writing in state schools, for example, might be deemed to be an ethical use of taxpayers money, if related test results, one year following its implementation, have improved. However, it is not out of the question that the benefits of the programme are ultimately confined to a handful of tests, and are merely short-term or medium-term. In fact, it might be that, long-term, the onerous or intensive nature of the programme has adversely impacted children's relationship with writing, leading to a lack of motivation and anxiety in adolescence, which contributes to young people being more likely to be persistently absent from school.

If we are to be truly teleological or consequentialist, therefore, when making decisions in the best interest of the majority, then we surely need to consider how far into the future we should be looking when linking these decisions to their apparent consequences. In relation to education, in my own view, we need to be mindful of the entire life course of children in classrooms, rather than their learning in the here and now. We also need to possibly be mindful of the world we are shaping, for future generations, and entire families, over time, through the actions that are undertaken in classrooms, playgrounds, and corridors, on a day-to-day basis.

Distinctions between short-term and long-term consequences of our actions also expose how utilitarianism could be used to legitimise opposing decisions in relation to SPMLD learners, arguably making it much more arbitrary and subjective than it alleges to be. Any utilitarian argument that it is detrimental to the majority to use public money on schooling those with SPMLD can actually also be contested from a utilitarian perspective. How can it be good for the majority to live in a world where the most vulnerable are shunned and denied an education? What positive impact does the education of learners with SPMLD bring to entire families and communities, and what is the price, to the majority in a society, of this impact, being lost? Can utilitarian arguments against schooling those with SPMLD ultimately be applied more broadly, to other marginalised groups, leading to a society which is deeply divided, and functioning only in the interest of an elite minority?

Even without the challenges associated with establishing what the ultimate consequences of our actions may be, even if we asserted that it is not in fact that difficult at all to calculate that a particular action or decision is likely to lead to positive outcomes for the majority, utilitarianism can still be easily criticised for undermining individual or minority rights. Unitarianism could be applied, for example, to legitimise a society in which a small proportion of the population serves as slaves. A high proportion of citizens in such a society may be happy about having access to free labour. However, it would be a considerable stretch to say that this makes slavery ethical. In his eighteenth-century writings, Jeremy Bentham, the founding father of utilitarianism, advocated for the forced incarceration of paupers in workhouses (Bentham, 2001). He argued that this would lead to enhanced happiness for the majority, who would rather not see beggars on the street whilst they were out walking. Along with those associated with the utilitarian argument for slavery, the striking flaws in Bentham's views highlight the varying extents to which different people may be impacted by an action. Can we say that a decision which we make is fair or just, when a majority of stakeholders in it are relatively nonchalant about any benefits which this brings them? Can we say that something is ethically the right thing to do, if it causes significant stress or harm to any individual?

Although the examples of slavery and workhouses are extreme and difficult to relate to decision-making relating to SPMLD in schools, the points that they raise, about individual rights and liberties, are applicable. Controversial approaches to modifying violent or sexualised behaviours, in a young adult with SLD, for example, may effectively benefit the majority by minimising the distress of peers, who may be disturbed by witnessing regular angry outbursts, and family members who might be struggling with the behaviours at home. However, these obvious benefits clearly need to be balanced with the needs of the individual. What is the threshold when supportive behaviour management strategies stop becoming supportive and become oppressive? From my personal perspective, it is important to establish such a threshold, regardless of the desires of the majority, and to ensure that it should never be crossed.

The Capabilities Approach

The Capabilities Approach is a philosophical framework with roots that can be traced back to utilitarianism. As discussed in the writings of Jeremy Bentham and John Stuart Mill, utilitarianism is hedonistic, being concerned with maximising pleasure and minimising pain. Similarly, the Capabilities Approach is focussed on maximising human 'flourishing' (Nussbaum, 2009, p. 345).

The Capabilities Approach, however, offers a much more nuanced perspective on ethical decision-making than the suggestion that we simply take actions that will lead to the greatest good for the greatest number of people. Unlike utilitarianism, it also starts with the assertion that human beings are 'ends not means' (Sen, 2001, p. 197), placing individual lives at the centre of decision-making, rather than as stopping points on a journey towards a perceived greater good. This assertion that human beings are 'ends not means,' enables us to rethink the purpose of education and challenge any arguments that schooling learners with PMLD is futile, if it does lead to them eventually contributing to the economy by joining the workforce and paying taxes. If we assume that human beings are 'ends not means,' then the purpose of education resides with the individuals being educated and their happiness.

The Capabilities Approach has its origins in development economics and in the writings of the Indian economist, Amartya Sen. In his seminal text 'Development as Freedom,' Sen prompts us to look beyond indicators such as the Gross Domestic Product (GDP) when evaluating the extent to which a nation-state has advanced or made progress. Rather than focus on GDP, he argues, we should also be looking at things such as civil liberties and democratic participation when undertaking such evaluations. Sen points out that there tends not to be famines in countries where democracies are strong, in which leaders are accountable to an electorate. Eliminating poverty, therefore, is not merely about increasing GDP or supplying food. It is about building just and ethical societies in which everyone, including those with SPMLD, can thrive.

The American Philosopher, Martha Nussbaum (2011) has built upon the work of Sen, and her writings provide an extremely valuable theoretical framework to support planning for learners with SPMLD in schools. In her version of the Capabilities Approach, she lists a set of ten central capabilities that respond to the question 'What are people able to do and be?'. The 'Ten Central Capabilities' are outlined in Figure 2.1 below and include

Figure 2.1 Nussbaum's set of 'Ten Central Capabilities.'

'affiliation' (being able to live and coexist with others), 'bodily health,' and 'play.' With this, it is noteworthy that the ten central capabilities in Nussbaum's list are not outlined in any hierarchy, and all have equal value. For example, 'practical reason' is not presented as a higher capability than 'bodily integrity.'

Nussbaum's writings have significant implications for decision-making around vulnerable learners in schools. Applying the Capabilities Approach, spending from a school budget, for an additional adult to join a school residential, for example, to enable the participation of an individual learner with medical needs, becomes the right thing to do. Although the other learners might benefit from the money being spent alternatively on a theatre visit during the week of the residential, or a bowling trip, they are already accessing and enjoying each of the ten central capabilities on Nussbaum's list, to a minmally acceptable level. In order to have 'bodily health' and 'bodily integrity,' however, to that minimally acceptable level, the individual learner with medical needs requires a care assistant to be away from home. To not have this care assistant would result in what has been referred to as 'capability deprivation' (Sen, 2001, p. 33). For the majority of learners, however, not having a theatre visit or a trip to a bowling alley wouldn't result in this. With reference to the Capabilities Approach, to passively say that we should make decisions in schools with the majority of pupils in mind, therefore, seems one-dimensional and avoids a deeper discussion around the *extent* to which decisions impact differently on different people.

The Capabilities Approach has also been applied to discussions around inclusive school curricula (Hedge and MacKenzie, 2012; Rogers, 2013; Price, 2015). As I have personally encountered across many schools that I have worked with, Nussbaum's set of ten central capabilities, for example, can serve as a framework for ensuring that children and young people with SPMLD have access to rich learning experiences that enable their holistic development. It is also possible for school leaders to map curriculum areas and topics against the capabilities that they support. Learning goals or targets can also be set, with each of the ten central capabilities in mind, to ensure that education provision is fully focussed on its ultimate purpose of fully enabling each child or young person to flourish.

Aristotelian Phronesis and Virtue Ethics

The Capability Approach is also an approach that could be broadly described as 'Aristotelian.' Both the Capability Approach and Aristotle's 'virtue ethics' emphasise human flourishing. From an Aristotelian perspective, to conduct ourselves ethically, we need to exercise virtues and behave in ways that cultivate these virtues, to enable our ongoing development as a person.

In his 'Eudemian Ethics' Aristotle (2017) identifies particular virtues that we should be practicing, as ethical beings, which include 'courage' and 'prudence'

(MacIntyre, 1966, pp. 66–69). In his writings, Aristotle also wrote about virtues residing at the 'Golden Mean' between two extremes. For example, 'truth' (or sincerity) is 'the Golden Mean' between 'self-depreciation' and 'boasting.' According to Aristotle, we become more virtuous through education, or through carrying out virtuous acts to enable us to become better at performing them (MacIntyre, 1966).

In education, frameworks or policies that emphasise professional values or dispositions could be seen as having much coherence with Aristotelian ethics. Efforts by school leaders to embed a set of such values, for example, through posters in staff areas and references to them across all planning documentation, could be seen as efforts to develop virtuous educators. In the context of the United Kingdom, the Association of School and College Leaders (Association of School and College Leaders, 2025) launched a 'Framework for Ethical Leadership in Education,' in 2017, which was the result of a year-long project that involved the mobilisation of an Ethical Leadership Commission. The 'Framework for Ethical Leadership in Education' outlines a set of characteristics for school leaders, which it refers to as 'virtues. These characteristics include 'justice,' 'courage,' and 'optimism.'

One possible criticism of Aristotelian 'virtue ethics' is that the presentation of two positions, as binary opposites, and extremities at each end of a spectrum, is highly subjective. An approach that could be extreme when placed on a continuum alongside some approaches would be moderate when placed alongside others. Another possible criticism is that there can be considerable ambiguity around any virtue. To permanently exclude a learner, for example, for persistent disruptive behaviour, against the protestations of professionals from outside the school, could be viewed as 'courageous.' Conversely, to refuse to exclude this learner and commit to supporting her, despite complaints from staff and concerns about resources, could alternatively be seen as the courageous thing to do. Central to Aristotelian ethics, however, is the virtue of 'phronesis,' which Florian and Graham (2014) explain as 'context-specific practical reasoning' (p. 467). We exercise the virtue of phronesis when we assess a situation in which we find ourselves and apply our learning from past situations to decide upon an appropriate course of action. Through phronesis, therefore, we make sense of any dilemmas that we find ourselves in and translate our wisdom into our responses to them. This notion of phronesis has parallels with the concept of 'Craft knowledge,' which underpins much of the research literature on inclusive practice in education (e.g., Florian and Graham, 2014).

For Aristotle, the development of phronesis is an 'iterative process' (Florian and Graham, 2014, p. 467) through which an individual engages in trial and reflection. In schools, professional learning activities such as dilemma-based coaching (Lofthouse, 2021), critical incident analysis (Tripp, 2012) or lesson study can facilitate this. These are discussed at length, in the final chapter of this book.

Kantian 'Duty Ethics'

According to Kakkori and Huttunen (2007), Aristotle's 'virtue ethics' can be largely contrasted with both utilitarian ethics and the ethics outlined by Immanuel Kant (1724–1804). Rather than 'virtue,' for example, Kantian 'duty' ethics associates ethical conduct with living according to certain rules or maxims.

Across his writings, Kant outlines his notion of the 'categorical imperative,' which is the idea that any actions that we take should be ones that we would wish to become a universal law (Sandel, 2010). This makes Kantian ethics diametrically opposed to utilitarianism, which instead asks us to calculate the anticipated consequences of our actions. Examples of categorical imperatives might include never dropping litter or endangering the life of another person. Whereas utilitarian ethics, therefore, is what we can refer to as 'teleological,' and looks to the future, Kantian ethics can be described as 'deontological' and is concerned with obligation and 'duty.' Unlike utilitarian ethics, Kant's writings also emphasise the idea that individual human beings are 'ends not means' that went on to also underpin the Capabilities Approach, which was formulated by Sen and Nussbaum in the twenty-first century.

Throughout my career in education, I have personally found Kantian assumptions underpinning professional dialogues on inclusion and exclusion in education. In my experience, for example, the word 'inclusion' has often been used to refer to the deontological principle that all pupils should go to a mainstream school and that there should be no special schools. From a more pragmatic or consequentialist perspective, we might appreciate that the local special school could be the best available option for 'Shona,' for example, who is regularly outside the classroom, in corridors, at her current mainstream setting. Also, from a consequentialist perspective, a utilitarian might then also argue that Shona's placement in a special school would mean that school staff were no longer spending a disproportionate amount of time attending to her needs, meaning that the majority of children and young people, in the mainstream school, benefit. Current education policy in Portugal, however, is not based on such arguments. The principle that every child should attend a mainstream school is a moral absolute. With this, it could be argued that it is only through adopting a deontological approach that inclusion in education can be effective. It could be argued that it is starting to be pragmatic, and making exceptions, that leads to exclusion and injustice.

Having coherence with the ideas of Kant, the notion of professional 'duty' can be easily found within schools. In the context of the United Kingdom, school staff are required to hold a 'duty of care' in relation to the children and young people they are serving. Safeguarding policies are also underpinned by core principles which reflect moral absolutes, that are deontological in nature and resonate with Kant's writings. Breaking confidentiality, by reporting disclosures of sexual abuse, for example, is not something that teachers and schools can waive on. To universally report such disclosures, therefore, whatever their context, is arguably underpinned by Kant's categorical imperative, as it is something that should always be followed. There is an obvious strong argument that, starting to deviate from this, by suggesting that teachers use their judgement to decide when to report a disclosure of sexual abuse, would be wholly inappropriate and lead to a reality where incorrect calls are made, to the detriment of vulnerable children. The exact same is the case with 'whistle-blowing' policies in schools, which require teachers to report serious concerns about the conduct of a colleague, which could impact the safety of pupils, such as using physical restraint disproportionately, or having pornographic websites in their browsing history, on classroom devices. Again, with this, school staff have an obligation, a duty. They must do what they must do, regardless of anything else.

With all of this in mind, the issue of whether or not it is ever acceptable to tell lies in schools (or stretch the truth) is also, in the context of Kant, a fascinating one. In discussing a Kantian approach to lying, Sandel (2010, p. 6) asks us to consider that a murderer has knocked on our door, looking for a friend who is inside our house, hiding from him. If we adopt a Kantian perspective and view that maxim 'Do not lie' as a universal rule that should never be broken, then surely we must tell the murderer the truth and answer the question 'Is Bob inside this building?' honestly. To put an insistence on never lying, however, above the safety of a friend, seems nonsensical and cruel.

Does professional practice with learners with SPMLD in schools always involve telling the truth? Are 'honesty' and 'transparency' absolute professional values that should always be adhered to and applied to any and every situation? From a Kantian perspective, we might argue that, to not have 'Tell the truth' as a universal law, it would mean a world in which teachers and school leaders are no longer respected by the community, and therefore trusted by children and young people, and their families. The social contract between schools and society would therefore break down. This argument might seem to be very utilitarian in nature. However, by emphasising the overall social contract, Kant is arguably proposing that the short-term consequences of an isolated action are insignificant in relation to the bigger picture of the society we want to live in.

Are there occasions, however, when lying within professional practice with learners with SPMLD is the correct thing to do? At times, in my own experience in schools, not telling an innocent lie would have potentially created situations and dynamics that would have most likely been unmanageable. We may not want to disclose the sexuality of a colleague, for example, to a parent with fundamentalist religious opinions who asks, 'Is Mr Fletcher gay?'. We may not want to give the actual reason why a class was short-staffed on a particular day, knowing that this would also disclose sensitive information that should not be in the public domain. Another tension, therefore, with Kantian ethics is that two different categorical imperatives can compete and clash. How can we universally abide by the maxim 'Do not lie?' and 'Always maintain confidentiality' simultaneously?

Positively, Kantian ethics does provide a philosophical framework to underpin contemporary notions of universal human rights. As pointed out by Sandel (2010, p. 103), it is much more difficult to advocate for universal human rights from a utilitarian perspective, which places the collective happiness of the majority above the freedom and dignity of the individual. Many schools, including schools with learners with SPMLD, are UNICEF 'Rights Respecting' Schools (UNICEF, 2025). This means that they have been awarded a quality mark for promoting and implementing the United Nations Convention on the Rights of the Child (UNCRC) within their school setting. The UNCRC has been signed by 196 countries and is legally binding. It incorporates 54 articles, each one outlining an entitlement that all persons under the age of 18 should be granted, unconditionally. Examples of articles include the right to be safe from violence (Article 19), the Right to an Education (Article 29), and the Right to Healthcare (Article 24). In relation to learners with SPMLD, being a UNICEF 'Rights Respecting' school, and being mindful of the articles in the UN Convention, may lead to greater attention being given, for example, to the views and opinions being expressed by those who may not have verbal communication. Helpfully, the UN Convention can support schools to outline some non-negotiables around the conditions for learning (e.g., in relation to safety) to ensure that they are not compromised or unconsciously disregarded amidst a busy school day.

However, in the same way as the categorical imperatives of 'Do not lie' and 'Always maintain confidentiality' can compete and clash, different articles within the UN Convention on the Rights of the Child can conflict with one another. Much has been written, for example, about how the right to protection from child labour (Article 32) could undermine the right of older children to secure safe, part-time work, as the only available means to ensure that themselves and their younger siblings can access education (Article 28), and an adequate standard of living (Article 27) (Collins and Wright, 2022). Conflicts between different articles within the UNCRC can also play out within education settings, with pupils with SPMLD. On one hand, for example, a school may be upholding Article 12 of the UNCRC (the right to express views) by supporting a learner with PMLD to choose between two photos of two different children, to indicate which one they would prefer to represent them on the school council. On the other hand, however, to put this learner through such a staged consultation process, with such limited awareness of what is going on, could be seen as a breach of Article 36, which is the right to protection from exploitation. Such tensions between different articles challenge a Kantian universal implementation of the same rules at all times and in all situations. Instead, they suggest a possible role for utilitarianism and/or the application of Aristotelian phronesis.

John Rawls and 'The Difference Principle'

According to the writings of John Rawls, we would be unlikely to choose utilitarianism as an ethical framework to live by if there were a significant likelihood of us being part of a marginalised group or oppressed minority. In his seminal work 'A Theory of Justice' (Rawls, 1972), Rawls presents us with his 'veil of ignorance' thought experiment, a hypothetical scenario to provoke reflection and discussion. He asks us to imagine that we have not yet been born, and do not know anything about the circumstances we will find ourselves in after birth (pp. 136–142). He asks us to imagine, for example, not knowing how much wealth our parents will have, or whether we will be born with any health difficulties. Wearing this 'veil of ignorance,' he points out, we would logically want a world where everybody can enjoy essential human rights and an adequate standard of living. We wouldn't want a world run for the benefit of the majority, knowing that there is a chance that we would not be in that majority. By imagining ourselves wearing the 'veil of ignorance,' therefore, we are considering what would be ultimately fair and just, rather than subjectively adopting a perspective which has been shaped by our levels of privilege and social status.

In his 'A Theory of Justice' Rawls addresses questions around whether-or-not it is acceptable for resources to be distributed unevenly, with some people enjoying greater wealth than others. Rawls rejects communism and the idea that each person in a society has exactly the same level of assets or income. However, Rawls also argues that it is only acceptable for some people to have more than others if the most vulnerable become better off as a consequence of this. Paying surgeons higher salaries, for example, might motivate people to train as surgeons, meaning that everybody, including those who are marginalised within society, benefits from having access to surgery, if and when they require it. This argument of Rawls, that inequality is permissible as long as this benefits the least fortunate, is known as 'The Difference Principle.'

The writings of Rawls can be used to strengthen ethical and moral arguments for investing in the education of learners with SPMLD. His 'veil of ignorance' thought experiment emphasises the injustice of a society where such investments are not made. Recently, I heard an account from a head teacher about parents making complaints following a summer concert due to concerns they had about children with visible disabilities performing alongside their own child who did not have any identified special educational needs. Comments from these parents included the abhorrent claim that their child risked becoming 'infected' by a disabled child. Although handing these parents a copy of Rawls 'Theory of Justice' may not have gone down well in this situation, it is arguably helpful for them to consider the possibility that we ourselves might have been born with SPMLD, or our own children might have been (as Rawls 'veil of ignorance' thought experiment might prompt us to). Considering this possibility, we would therefore be unlikely to put forward any utilitarian argument that schooling these learners, or having them perform in a school concert, was detrimental to the majority. Instead, we would assert their right to be included.

In his writings, Rawls challenges the notion of 'meritocracy' that is central to liberalism (pp. 106–108). This is the idea that a person's success within a society should be based 'on merit' rather than on the family they are born into. At first hand, this principle of meritocracy feels difficult to disagree with. According to Rawls, however, the suggestion that ascribed 'merit' is the basis for human advancement assumes that particular individuals lack merit and have a natural place in the lower echelons of society. In relation to those with SPMLD, therefore, the idea of meritocracy seems to legitimise low incomes and levels of poverty within their families, which may arise from low rates of benefits such as Disability Living Allowance in England, and costs associated with care, such as taxis, cleaning equipment, and nappies. Rawls prompts us to ask why we think it is ethically justifiable to reward those deemed to possess merit with higher salaries and social status, when they did not personally choose or shape the circumstances that awarded them their position in society. Assuming that the wealthy and those in senior job roles truly deserve to have more than others, Rawls argues, is not the basis for justice.

Nel Noddings and 'Care Ethics'

Noddings was a philosopher with a background in teaching in American schools. From the perspective of educational philosophy, her writings outline an 'ethics of care' (Noddings, 2013, p. 50). Nodding argues that when approaching decision-making in schools, we should consider which action would most effectively strengthen our relationships with our learners. Rather than considering the greatest good, for the greatest number of people, as utilitarians do, we should consider what would most effectively nurture this 'caring relation' (Noddings, 2013, p. 42).

In her writings, Noddings (2005) also outlines a distinction between the 'expressed' needs of learners, and the needs of learners that are 'inferred' by adults (p. 148). Through actively working to strengthen the caring relation in the classroom, as educators, she argues, we will be better equipped to responding to learners' expressed needs. Without attention to this caring relation however, we are merely working with abstract and hypothetical notions of what the needs of our learners are, which are inferred from what we think we know and understand. To conduct ourselves ethically in the classroom therefore, we need to communicate with our learners and gain greater insight into the needs they are expressing, whilst recognising the inevitable misconceptions underpinning our inferences about what their needs might be.

In my experience, in school settings with learners with SPMLD, adults tend to sit around the table in meetings and talk about activities that an individual apparently 'enjoys,' as well as further opportunities that they are perceived to 'need,' to enable them to flourish. It might be said, for example, that 'Hannah likes doing hair and make-up with the girls from Jupiter Class,' or 'Toseef likes watching the football on the TV, with his brothers.' It might also be advised in such meetings that Hannah needs a picture-supported communication system, or that Toseef needs to be discouraged from talking about the film 'Toy Story.' Whereas these things, for Hannah and Toseef, might be entirely valid, it can be helpful for the meeting to consider whether any stated needs are based on what these two young people are expressing themselves, or if they are merely being inferred. Is Hannah's communication and cognition actually at the level, for example, where she is able to access small, laminated pictures, and recognise them as representations of objects within her classroom? Does she have the fine motor skills to scroll through these pictures in a small book? How do we know that Toseef enjoys football? What responses do we look for to establish that he is experiencing enjoyment when watching a game? Are the conclusions we are making in relation to Emily and Toseef an outcome of a 'caring relation'? Or are they conclusions that are based on what the adults in the meeting in fact need, to demonstrate professionalism, for example, or to emulate perceived normality?

Nodding's distinction between expressed needs and inferred needs can also be helpful in relation to curriculum design for learners with SPMLD. At earlier points in my own career as a school leader, I have personally been actively involved in the creation and dissemination of what has been referred to, within schools, as 'needs-based' curricula. Typically, such curricula will be made up of alternative curriculum areas that are different from the traditional school subjects in the National Curriculum, such as English, Maths, and Science. A curriculum that has been designed for learners with Severe Learning Difficulties, for example, might include curriculum areas related to developing independent living skills, such as 'How My World Works' and 'Accessing the Community.' A curriculum designed for learners with Profound and Learning and Difficulties might be termed a 'sensory curriculum,' with the aim of stimulating engagement or responsiveness. On one hand, these needs-based curricula arguably offer a framework to teachers and schools to support the planning of rich learning experiences that are developmentally appropriate for those with SPMLD. On the other hand, it is helpful for us to ask ourselves whether-or-not the needs that they are based on are those that are subjectively being inferred. There is an argument that there will be an inevitable dissonance between the needs of hypothetical and/or generic learners with SLD, that an 'SLD Curriculum' has been designed around, and the actual needs of the actual learners with SLD, in our classrooms.

Conclusion

As demonstrated in the above discussion, ethical theory offers valuable intellectual tools to those working with learners with SPMLD in schools. This theory can be applied to enrich discussions and challenge established patterns of thinking. From my own perspective, teachers and school leaders do not necessarily need to choose a particular theory to consistently subscribe to, with fidelity. Despite its clear limitations in relation to SPMLD learners, teachers and schools do not need to universally reject utilitarianism, for example, or subscribe to the Capabilities Approach, to the exclusion of ethical theories that are deemed to contradict it. Instead, schools can allow an awareness of ethical theories to challenge previously taken-for-granted assumptions and recognise their imperfections.

References

Aristotle. (2017). *The Eudemian Ethics of Aristotle Translated with Explanatory Comments by Peter L.P. Simpson* (E-Book Viewer). London: Routledge.

Association of School and College Leaders (2025 19th May). Framework for ethical leadership in education. Retrieved from https://www.ascl.org.uk/ASCL/media/ASCL/Our%20view/Campaigns/Framework-for-Ethical-Leadership-in-Education.pdf

Bentham, J. (2001). *The Collected Works of Jeremy Bentham: Writings on the Poor Laws, Vol. 1*. Oxford University Press. https://doi.org/10.1093/actrade/9780199242320.book.1

Collins, T. M., & Wright, L. H. V. (2022). The challenges for children's rights in international child protection: Opportunities for transformation. *World Development, 159*. https://doi.org/10.1016/j.worlddev.2022.106032

Education Endowment Foundation (2025, 19th May). Evidence and resources. Retrieved from https://educationendowmentfoundation.org.uk/education-evidence

Florian, L., & Graham, A. (2014). Can an expanded interpretation of phronesis support teacher professional development for inclusion? *Cambridge Journal of Education, 44*(4). https://doi.org/10.1080/0305764X.2014.960910

Hedge, N., & MacKenzie, A. (2012). Putting Nussbaum's Capability Approach to work: Re-visiting inclusion. *Cambridge Journal of Education, 42*(3). https://doi.org/10.1080/0305764X.2012.706252

Kakkori, L., & Huttunen, R. (2007). Aristotle and pedagogical ethics. *Paideusis, 16*(1). https://doi.org/10.7202/1072603ar

Lofthouse, R. (2021 20 April). *Exploring and Learning from Educational Complexity Through Dilemma-Based Coaching*. Leeds Beckett University. Retrieved from https://www.leedsbeckett.ac.uk/blogs/carnegie-education/2021/04/exploring-and-learning-from-educational-complexity/

MacIntyre, A. (1966). *A Short History of Ethics* (1st ed.). New York: Macmillan.

Noddings, N. (2013). *Caring: A Relational Approach to Ethics and Moral Education* (2nd ed.). California: University of California Press.

Noddings, N. (2005). Identifying and responding to needs in education. *Cambridge Journal of Education, 35*(2), 147–159. https://doi.org/10.1080/03057640500146757

Nussbaum, M. (2009). The capabilities of people with cognitive disabilities. *Metaphilosophy, 40*(3–4). https://doi.org/10.1111/j.1467-9973.2009.01606.x

Nussbaum, M. (2011). *Creating Capabilities: The Human Development Approach*. The Belknap Press of Harvard University Press.

Price, D. (2015). Pedagogies for inclusion of students with disabilities in a national curriculum: A central human capabilities approach. *Journal of Educational Enquiry, 14*(2).

Rawls, J. (1972). *A Theory of Justice*. Oxford University Press.

Rogers, C. (2013). Inclusive education and intellectual disability: A sociological engagement with Martha Nussbaum. *International Journal of Inclusive Education*, *17*(9), 988–1002. https://doi.org/10.1080/13603116.2012.727476

Sandel, M. J. (2010). *Justice: What's the Right Thing To Do?* London: Penguin Books.

Sen, A. (2001). *Development as Freedom*. Oxford: Oxford University Press.

van Toorn, G., Henhan, P., & Soldatic, K. (2024). Introduction to the digital welfare state: Contestations, considerations and entanglements. *Journal of Sociology*, *60*(3), 507–522.

Tripp, D. (2012). *Critical Incidents in Teaching: Developing Professional Judgement* (Classical Edition). London: Routledge.

UK Gov. (2025, 6th May). *Special Educational Needs in England*. Available at: https://explore-education-statistics.service.gov.uk/find-statistics.special-educational-needs-in-england/2023-24

UNICEF UK. (2025, 10 May). *Rights Respecting Schools: Putting Child Rights at the Heart of School Life*. Available at: https://www.unicef.org.uk/rights-respecting-schools/

Watson, K. (2024, 8th July). 'You're not welcome here': Australia's treatment of disabled migrants. *BBC News*. https://www.bbc.co.uk/news/articles/cyr70ezev2mo

Chapter 3

SPMLD, theories of learning, and debates

In addition to there being a variety of perspectives on the issue of where children with SPMLD are taught, there are also a variety of perspectives on a range of other issues. This chapter explores these issues and discusses a series of key questions which underpin debates relating to the schooling of those with SPMLD, that are central to decision-making around pedagogy, policy, and strategy.

What Should Learners with SPMLD Be Taught?

There is a wide range of perspectives on what learners with SPMLD should be taught and what learning goals are appropriate. Across different schools and national contexts, curricula for learners with SPMLD can vary enormously.

One key area of contention, in relation to curriculum for learners with SPMLD, is around whether traditional national curriculum subjects, such as Science and History, offer anything purposeful to them. On one hand, it is often argued that there are essential areas of learning, which all children, in any school system, have a fundamental right to access, because they represent the foundations of education, and for success in life. There have been active campaigns in England, for example, for all children, whatever their need or diagnosis, to have the opportunity to be taught how to read and write. Such campaigns are largely associated with a young man called Jonathan Bryan, who sadly passed away in June 2025, at the age of 19, just as this book was going into production. Through the charity 'Teach Us Too' (Teach Us Too, 2025), Jonathan and his family advocated for the teaching of literacy to all learners in schools, regardless of their label. Jonathan was a wheelchair user with cerebral palsy, who communicated by spelling out words on an alphabet board, held in front of him, by using his eyes. In his book, 'Eye Can Write' (2018), he gave an account of his early schooling in a specialist setting. Within this setting, by being given the label 'PMLD,' he was placed on a 'sensory curriculum' that was deemed to best meet his needs. Such curricula, in Jonathan's view, reflected low expectations of PMLD learners and denied them the educational entitlements that they deserve.

DOI: 10.4324/9781003540106-5

Those arguing for alternative curricula, for those with SPMLD, may point out that a child at Jonathan's level of functioning should not have been given the label 'PMLD' in the first place. Rather than have a profound intellectual disability, they would assert, Jonathan started school with profound barriers to learning, associated with physical disabilities. Whereas there would be a great injustice in not teaching children how to read, on the basis of them having multiple physical disabilities, it would arguably also be unjust to subject those with profound intellectual disabilities to phonics sessions, when they could be being supported to reach developmental milestones (such as expressing preferences for particular stimuli) that offer the most significant enhancements to their long-term wellbeing. Such arguments for alternative curricula are based on an alternative conceptualisation of the notion of 'entitlement,' in the context of education. Under this conceptualisation, learners are viewed as not all having an entitlement to the same core offer of a national curriculum, but as having an entitlement to be met at their particular point of learning and having access to opportunities that are meaningful. For a five-year-old with a physical disability, without PMLD, it is meaningful to be taught how to read. For a learner with PMLD (so the argument goes), it isn't. If we do not consider it appropriate to teach strategies for decoding words to a 3-week-old baby, then it is surely also not appropriate for a 12-year-old learner, at an analogous developmental level.

In my own professional experience, merely adapting national curriculum subjects such as History for learners with SPMLD has often been for the benefit of teachers and schools, to demonstrate their accountability, rather than for the benefit of the learners themselves. At their worst, I have found attempts to make national curriculum subjects accessible for learners with SPMLD to be harmful and dehumanising. For example, I once encountered how the requirements for a formal certification programme related to Geography included 'Wear a Mexican hat.' Such requirements inevitably compel classroom staff to dress learners up and take photos to go into a 'skills folder' or portfolio, ignoring any discomfort they may be experiencing, and undermining the more important goals of maximising independence and agency. If this is what 'entitlement' to the national curriculum for all learners becomes, then what is the point? Whose interests are we really serving? Are we actually even providing what could be called 'education'?

Within the field of special educational needs, therefore, there are some very strong advocates for more alternative curriculum frameworks, who have made significant and valuable contributions to collective thinking around the schooling of those with SPMLD. Imray and Hinchcliffe (2013), for example, challenge the view that the national curriculum is suitable for all learners. They also outline some possible alternative subjects, or learning areas, that could be included within a needs-based curriculum for learners with SLD. Examples of these alternative learning areas include 'Communication,' 'Physical Development,' and

'Problem Solving and Thinking Skills.' In the context of England, a significant number of specialist school settings have devised a range of curriculum pathways, which typically include an adapted national curriculum for learners with Moderate Learning Difficulties (MLD), a curriculum focused on developing life skills for learners with SLD, and a sensory curriculum for learners with PMLD. This indeed was the model that I led the development of as a senior leader in the 2010s, at Swiss Cottage School in London, which was one of the first special schools in England to take the brave step of departing from the wholesale adoption of the national curriculum. As a browse through school websites shows, such curriculum pathways tend to determine timetabling, the formation of departments within the school, and the establishment of particular job roles. A school for example, may have a team of teachers within it, who form the 'Sensory Curriculum Team,' that is led by a 'Head of PMLD Provision.'

One argument for alternative needs-based curricula for learners with complex SEND is that they label curriculum areas and learning experiences more honestly (Imray and Hinchcliffe, 2012, 2013; Byers and Lawson, 2015). Rather than pretend that pupils with SLD, for example, are doing 'Geography' when they go to visit local shops, it can be argued that it may be more sensible to instead frame the activity around 'Communication' or one of the other crucial areas being addressed through a more needs-based, alternative developmental curriculum. This argument would be supported by the suggestion that it is, in fact, deep learning that all learners have an entitlement to. This is the idea that learners should be offered experiences which go beyond surface-level learning to enable full immersion and a state of 'flow' (West-Burnham and Coates, 2005). The emphasis on the growing distinctiveness of special education from mainstream schooling, from authors such as Imray and Hinchcliffe (2012, 2013) seems to represent a call to bring deep learning to those pupils who may only otherwise be touching the surface of subjects such as Modern Foreign Languages or Geography.

With a subject such as Geography, a group of pupils with PMLD may benefit enormously from an activity on 'Water in the Village,' which involves a lot of messy play with sand. However, there is likely to remain some disconnect between individual pupils' experience of this activity, the subtext of global themes and issues within the mind of the teacher who planned the session. Although the activity on 'Water in the Village' may develop higher levels of engagement in some pupils, we need to be cautious before we claim that through it, we are doing Geography. This is similar to the arguments made by Imray and Hinchcliffe (2012, 2013) and the associated suggestion that we need to be cautious before claiming that, through other activities in special schools, we are doing subjects such as History or Science. Ultimately, it could be damaging to pupils with SPMLD to claim that we are covering particular areas of learning through activities, which actually only touch the surface of them.

Are Specialist Curricula Preferable?

It could easily be argued that the design of a specialist sensory curriculum, for learners with PMLD, or the design of a 'Independent Living Skills' curriculum, for learners with 'Severe Learning Difficulties' (with their own alternative subject areas, which are different from national curriculum subject areas), is by no means unproblematic. I have personally found, for example, that there can be a huge dissonance between the imagined 'PMLD learner' that a sensory curriculum has been constructed around, and the real learners with the label 'PMLD' in real classrooms. This can especially be the case when such a curriculum is shared between schools or marketed as a commercial product. As those with 'PMLD' represent such an exceptionally diverse cohort, a curriculum suitable for learners with this label in one classroom context may offer little value to learners with PMLD in another. I have also personally found huge variations in how the terms 'SLD' and 'PMLD' are used, in different schools, and within different local authorities. A learner who may be seen to have SLD alongside a physical disability may be placed on a curriculum for those with SLD in one setting, for example. Her family could then relocate to another area and be placed on a sensory curriculum for learners with PMLD.

In my own experience, it is very easy for needs-based curricula, for learners with SLD or PMLD, to be shaped by outdated stereotypes and assumptions of commonality across what are in fact extremely heterogeneous learner populations. With all their uniqueness, individuals carrying the label 'SLD' or 'PMLD' tend to defy these stereotypes beautifully. Curricula developed for learners with 'PMLD' or 'SLD' can also be based on what Nodding (2005) refers to as 'inferred needs' (p. 148). For Nodding's 'inferred needs' are those that we assume learners to have, based on our uninformed, subjective impressions of them. Rather than work with 'inferred needs,' she argues, we need to be working with 'expressed needs,' which we elicit through building a 'caring relation' (2013, p. 32) with learners, through our teaching. There is an argument that the process of implementing any alternative, specialist curriculum for learners with SLD or PMLD actually undermines practitioner interaction with expressed needs. It could be claimed that such alternative curricula focus teachers on simplistic hypotheticals rather than on the complex realities at play in their classrooms.

Also, in my own experience, a school could develop (for example) three different curriculum pathways around the labels of 'Moderate Learning Difficulties,' 'Severe Learning Difficulties,' and 'Profound and Multiple Learning Difficulties' yet have very many learners who cannot neatly be placed into any one of them. I have come across schools that have responded to this issue by devising even more curricula, such as one for learners whose needs may be perceived as falling between 'Moderate Learning Difficulties' and 'Severe Learning Difficulties.' Rather than help, I have personally found that such solutions have tended to complicate things further, and lead to more generalisations being made, and more stereotyping. In recent years, I have come across educators who have added to a 'three curricula' model by creating a fourth (and sometimes a fifth, sixth, or seventh) curriculum within their setting. With this, I often wonder whether or not the further development of more-and-more needs-based curriculum models within a school can logically ever stop, given how inevitable it seems that teachers will continue to encounter learners who challenge professional perceptions of each of the perceived 'SEND groups' underpinning each one. Whereas I was once so committed to strengthening personalisation of learning through developing a menu of specialist curricula, I now ask myself whether or not it would be more appropriate to advocate for a more singular, universal offer of education that is sufficiently flexible to support everyone.

Through interviews with teachers of learners with PMLD, Stewart and Walker-Gleaves (2020, p. 353) found a 'continuum of therapeutic to disciplinary curricula' across different specialist settings in the United Kingdom. Whereas some settings have a curriculum based on national curriculum subjects, which emulates mainstream education, other settings organise the school day around more holistic curriculum areas, aligned with more developmental goals being also addressed by social care and healthcare practitioners. Whatever the curriculum policy within their schools, however, Stewart and Walker-Gleaves also found that, behind the closed door of their classroom, teachers of those with PMLD tended to quietly rebel, and deliver what made sense to them, for their learners, regardless. As well as there being considerable variation in approaches to curriculum between schools, their research revealed a 'nexus of curriculum-pedagogical politics' (p.356), around which it was difficult to establish any consensus.

Stewart's and Walker-Gleaves' research seems to highlight how curriculum redesign for learners with SPMLD may not be the lever for change, which school leaders and self-proclaimed experts in the field may view it to be. There is a huge difference, we could argue, between the written curriculum, with its various flow charts and illustrative tables, and the curriculum that learners with PMLD are experiencing. Arguably, therefore, rather than investment in curriculum redesign, it is instead effective leadership and the granting of professional agency to teachers that offers the most significant positive impact on learners. Within an appropriate school culture, it could be claimed, the teaching of national curriculum subjects could authentically enrich the development of SPMLD pupils. Within a culture focussed on accountability and compliance, however, an alternative developmental curriculum could fall into the same performative practices, which I had found, in my career, to often accompany the teaching of national curriculum subjects such as Geography or History. Just as requiring a learner with PMLD to 'Wear a Mexican Hat' in Geography could ultimately be pointless and disrespectful, positioning them next to a dishwasher, to pose for a photo, in a lesson on 'Independent Living Skills,' could be the same. Any curriculum, therefore, whatever the rationale behind it, and however logical it might appear on paper, is only as good as the ways in which it is translated and enacted on a daily basis.

What Do We Mean by 'SPMLD Pedagogy'?

Beyond curriculum, there are ongoing dialogues around how exactly teachers of those with SPMLD should plan and organise learning and deliver learning activities. By bringing unique ways of learning into classrooms, for example, learners with SPMLD, in my experience, challenge pedagogical conventions and assumptions around what teaching and learning in classrooms should 'look like.' A range of specialist pedagogical approaches has also been developed for specific groups of learners, and debates persist around their appropriateness and value.

The term pedagogy has been defined as 'the act of teaching together with its attendant discourses' (Alexander, 2004, p. 11). Pedagogy, therefore, involves the delivery of teaching methods and approaches, underpinned by a rationale for using them. When teaching children to read, for example, we might adopt a pedagogical approach based on systematic synthetic phonics and, in explaining this, we may refer to concepts such as grapheme-phoneme correspondence, which is the capacity to match a sound to its written representation. When teaching maths, our pedagogy might be based on the use of concrete manipulatives (physical objects), for example, to teach different ways of making the number ten, or the concept of division.

In relation to learners with SPMLD, an important starting point for exploring pedagogy would be to consider questions around the extent to which it varies according to who, or what, we are teaching. If we are teaching counting to 10, it could easily be argued that then we may use a similar combination of number lines, songs, and matching activities, whether our learners have special educational needs or not. Whatever we are teaching, and to whom, we may consider it good practice to build formative assessment activities into a session, to enable us to elicit what has been achieved and what priorities need to be addressed in the next session. We may, or may not, also consider it an appropriate pedagogical strategy to build community and collaboration within our classrooms and create opportunities for interaction.

Discussions around what may constitute 'SPMLD pedagogy,' therefore (and around whether or not there is actually such a thing) relate back to considerations around the extent to which teaching these learners is dissimilar to teaching anyone else. Can we say that all teaching is teaching, regardless of who we have in our classrooms? Or are there specialisms within teaching that effectively make educating learners with SPMLD an entirely different job to (for example) teaching Science in a mainstream secondary school? Such considerations require us to explore our perspectives on what resides at the very heart of the teaching profession. In relation to this, the emphasis on teaching itself being a learning activity, which is emphasised in the European Agency for the Development of Special Needs Education 'Profile of Inclusive Teachers' (EADSNE, 2012) may be helpful. If we do consider teaching to be a leaning activity, and a dynamic process through which teachers glean new insights into learners and learning, which they then respond to through their ongoing planning, then we are surely also assuming that it is the more universal professional qualities of teachers, that make the most difference, rather than any pre-prepared specialist skills for particular classroom contexts. Saying this, my experience tells me that if a Science teacher from a mainstream school attempted to teach a class of learners with SPMLD in the exact same way as they deliver secondary Science lessons, they would most likely not get very far!

Do Learners with SPMLD Ever Benefit from Whole Class Teaching?

One frequent discussion I have encountered globally, around pedagogy for learners with SPMLD, is around the purpose and value of whole class teaching. Does it necessarily make sense for a group of nine learners with SLD to sit around a table together, all working on the same task, and following the same directions? As much as this is an important question to ask, reaching an answer to it, for me, does not feel particularly difficult. It depends entirely on who those learners with SLD are, their developmental level, and their priorities for learning. I would personally confidently assert that pedagogy for learners with SPMLD cannot ever be around absolutes, and that general questions such as 'Should learners with SLD ever be taught as a whole class?' are unhelpful, with teachers needing to instead address questions about what is appropriate pedagogy for their own learners.

Whether we decide that whole class teaching is ever suitable for learners with SPMLD, there are clear moral arguments for thinking beyond such conventions and taken-for-granted assumptions around what teaching and learning 'should' look like. In my own career, I remember once working with three boys, aged between 8 and 11, who each had the label 'PMLD.' These boys had a very similar profile to one another. All three had no spoken language and very rarely made eye contact with anyone. Cognitively and developmentally, they were not yet at a stage where they could feed themselves or use a toilet. However, unlike the other children in their class, these three boys were not wheelchair users and would independently walk around the classroom, picking up (and often licking) objects that they found. In order to support their learning, therefore, their teacher strategically placed various resources around the space, for them to find, including materials with different textures and smells, as well as equipment that they could control with a button (or 'switch' device), to support them to begin to link cause and effect. This allowed classroom staff to be opportunistic when nurturing the holistic development of the three boys. They would follow the boys as they wandered, modelling language and facial expressions in response to various stimuli they showed an interest in, and/or demonstrating how things worked. This approach seemed to be effective in strengthening their curiosity and overall engagement. However, it was an entirely different approach to the one insisted upon by a previous head teacher, who argued that, when they were wandering about, the boys were 'off-task' and 'not working.' This head teacher expected the classroom practitioners to arrange all seven learners in the class into a circle for activities such as storytelling sessions or singing. When they were not in a circle, she expected the three boys to be sitting at a table, doing a matching activity, even if this meant being strapped into a chair or a teaching assistant using 'hand-over-hand' to get them to match correctly. From the head teacher's perspective, this was in the best interests of the three boys and meant that they were not losing out on an education. In reality, however, the approach that she insisted on seemingly compromised their learning and development, making the boys less curious and more passive.

Although the above anecdote may initially come across as extreme, it is by no means an unfamiliar one in my own experience. It is an anecdote which prompts important thinking around pedagogy for learners with SPMLD, as well as highlighting how teaching and learning for these learners may inevitably need to 'look different.' It may involve the classroom being 'zoned' into different areas, for example, in which two learners may be on the carpet with a teaching assistant, enjoying a story, and others may be sat around a table, painting, and one may be sat with an iPad with his feet in a tray of sand, preparing for an upcoming holiday by visiting a beach virtually.

The above anecdote, however, about the three boys, is also an anecdote which highlights what can happen when universal and essential characteristics of effective pedagogy are missing. A culture of responsive teaching, for example, based on the information about learning gleaned through observations and/or formative assessments (which is what, in my view, characterises good teaching in any context, including mainstream secondary) would have likely enabled the head teacher to ultimately notice the negative impact that whole class teaching was having.

To What Extent Can Specialist Pedagogies Support the Teaching of Learners with SPMLD?

A wide array of specialist pedagogies is available to teachers and schools. These include subject-specific pedagogies for teaching particular areas of the curriculum and pedagogies that have been developed with specific groups of learners or needs in mind. A possible example of a specialist pedagogy associated with autism education might be 'Applied Behavioural Analysis' (ABA), which involves conditioning an individual to learn how to behave in ways that are deemed to be acceptable, through a system of positive and negative reinforcement (American Psychological Association, 2017). Another, very different example, which is arguably based on entirely different values to ABA, is

'Attention Autism' (Davies, 2025), which is a playful approach to developing motivation, creativity, and shared enjoyment within a community of learners. An example of a specialist pedagogy associated with the teaching of learners with Profound and Multiple Learning Difficulties might include 'TACPAC,' which is based on the use of touch and music to build communication with a learner. That all of these things could be referred to as 'pedagogies,' however, is contestable, depending on the stance taken on curriculum for SPMLD learners, and boundaries between therapy and education.

The dissemination of specialist pedagogies is also often supported by research that supports claims that they are 'evidence-based.' The credibility of the 'TEACCH' approach, for example (which still continues to refer to itself as 'Treatment and Education of Autistic and Related Communication Handicapped Children'), developed for autism education, is underpinned by the findings of multiple research studies. In a meta-analysis of these studies (Zhou et al., 2024), an evidence-based approach was presented, suggesting that single components of the TEACCH approach (such as the use of visual timetables and individual workstations for learners) are generally effective in maximising engagement.

Usually, specialist pedagogies can be accessed by teachers and schools through products such as training courses, consultancy packages, and manuals. In a 2015 article, Jones & Lawson (2015), describe how, in the US State of Florida, evidence-based pedagogies have led to the proliferation of 'commercial packages' relating to specialist pedagogies, for teaching learners with particular special educational needs, which teachers are 'obliged to take on' (p. 395). Quite often, in my experience, it is learners with SPMLD who are at the centre of this 'deluge of education Do-It-Yourself manuals' and 'tip texts' which, according to Slee (2013: pp. 895–896) merely offer 'quick fixes'.

In contributing to debates around specialist and inclusive pedagogies, systematic literature reviews and meta-studies over the years have also found that it is very generic teaching qualities, based on broad notions of 'good teaching,' that tend to be most associated with the practice of specialist SEND teachers. Lewis and Norwich (2007), for example, reviewed literature relating to teaching pupils with a range of different diagnoses and found much commonality between the strategies cited and those strategies that underpin high-quality teaching for any learner in the school system, such as 'more practice to achieve mastery' (Lewis and Norwich, 2007, p. 132). In their 2007 publication 'Special Teaching for Special Children?', distinct strategies were only found by Norwich and Lewis, in relation to the teaching of learners with difficulties with sight or hearing (Lewis and Norwich, 2007). An international study conducted by Rix et al. (in Rix and Sheehy 2014, p. 3) reached similar conclusions and found that the following approaches for teaching pupils with special educational needs were referred to within the literature, which featured in their analysis:

- *modifying environment*
- *differentiated pedagogy*

- *activities to promote individual learning*
- *diversified materials and resources*
- *use of Braille*
- *use of signed communication*
- *use of symbols*
- *use of interpreters*
- *activities with peers*
- *increased use of computers/ICT*
- *team teaching*
- *visual, technical, demonstrational means, computer software, toys, objects and materials and exercise books.*

(Rix, Sheehy, Fletcher-Campbell, Crisp & Harper, 2013 in Rix and Sheehy, 2014, p. 3)

It has been argued that an emphasis on special pedagogies for 'special' learners can actually be harmful. Much has also been written about how a focus on specialist pedagogies can undermine the confidence of teachers by suggesting to them that they are unable to teach particular pupils because they haven't been trained in the requisite knowledge and skills (Florian and Rouse, 2010; Rix and Sheehy, 2014). According to Florian and Rouse (2010) such a focus can lead teachers to 'believe that there are experts "out there" to deal with these students on a one-to-one basis or in small groups' (Florian and Rouse, 2010, p. 190) rather than trust that they have what it takes within their skill set, to address the barriers to learning experienced by their pupils. It is certainly my own experience that specialist SEND approaches can undermine teachers' feelings of self-efficacy. Throughout my career, for example, it has not been unusual at all to encounter teachers who do not feel that they have been trained to teach a particular class because they haven't been on a particular course on a particular diagnosis-specific method, only to feel empowered and inspired once they have given it a go. I have also encountered situations where the purchase of a manual relating to a specialist pedagogy, or attendance on a course, has undermined interactive teaching. In such situations, teachers had been reduced to passive transmitters of specialist methods, leading them to a focus on fidelity to these methods, rather than on the learners themselves.

Does the Principle of Inclusive Pedagogy Have Anything to Offer Learners with SPMLD?

A commitment to the principle of Inclusive Pedagogy can broadly be contrasted with a commitment to a focus on dispensing specialist pedagogies deemed appropriate for particular diagnoses and labels.

Central to the definition of Inclusive Pedagogy is the notion of 'extending what is ordinarily available for all learners rather than using teaching and learning strategies that are suitable for most alongside something 'additional' or 'different' for those who experience difficulties' (Black-Hawkins and Florian 2012, p. 575). Rather than the setting of different activities for 'some' and 'most' learners (Spratt and Florian, 2014, p. 129) an inclusive pedagogical approach begins with considerations around how the overall learning environment and core learning tasks can be enhanced to enable greater access for everybody. An example of 'extending what is ordinarily available to all,' in the context of a mainstream primary school, might be the use of story props during story-time, along with other multi-sensory stimuli, to address numerous barriers to participation, including working memory difficulties, attention difficulties, and difficulties around processing language. Inclusive Pedagogy therefore represents a departure from learners having separate, differentiated activities dispensed to them, on the basis of their perceived ability.

It is difficult, if not impossible, to apply the notion of 'extending what is ordinarily available to all' to classrooms with learners with SPMLD. Although extending the range of available multi-sensory stimuli may occasionally make joining a story telling session, alongside those without SPMLD, accessible to some of these learners, no amount of enhancements to what is 'ordinarily available' (I have found through my own practice) will enable them to meaningfully engage with activities that they are not developmentally ready for. As the overwhelming majority of learners globally, who may be identified with 'SPMLD,' do not attend mainstream schools, it is unsurprising that they tend not to feature in published studies on inclusive education. However, this absence, which has been acknowledged in the academic literature (Colley, 2020), highlights how the 'all,' that is emphasised in definitions of Inclusive Pedagogy, may not actually mean 'all' in reality.

Despite these highly significant issues, it can still validly be argued that tenets of the inclusive pedagogical approach, in fact, do have some applicability to the teaching of learners with SPMLD. For example, the emphasis of the research literature on Inclusive Pedagogy, on getting the overall social conditions and dynamics within a classroom right (e.g., Spratt and Florian, 2014, p. 90), rather than on merely matching tasks to children, is arguably something that can be applied to optimising the learning experience of those with SPMLD. There is much coherence between the notion of Inclusive Pedagogy and socio-cultural theories of learning, which focus on the 'complex web of social relations' within a classroom (Spratt and Florian, 2015, p. 90). The psychologist Vygotsky (1896–1934) has made many key contributions to socio-cultural theories of learning. These are discussed, for example, by Daniels (2009), who relates Vygotsky's ideas to considerations for the implementation of inclusive classroom practice. For Vygotsky, learning is dialogical, occurring through meaningful communication (Daniels, 2009, p. 28). This makes Vygotsky's theories distinct from those of Piaget (1896–1980), who instead maintained that young children first progress through sequential developmental phases through self-discovery, before being ready for more formal education. Vygotsky's perspective is also distinct from the behaviourist perspective of Skinner (1904–1990), who argued that children receive knowledge from teachers through direct instruction (Daniels, 2009, pp. 26–27). According to Vygotskian theories, it is instead the absence of the 'zone of proximal development' (ZPD) that reduces the capacity for learning (Daniels, 2009). It is within the ZPD that a learner exceeds what they can achieve independently and grows through interaction with others, including 'knowledgeable other(s)' such as peers within a class or their teacher(s). For Vygotsky, therefore, children with disabilities, who are educated away from others, develop 'secondary disabilities' caused through social deprivation, the absence of an effective ZPD, and limited meaningful communication with others (Daniels 2009, pp. 32–33).

For some learners with PMLD, engaging in the independent exploration of a learning environment, to move through various developmental stages sequentially, in the ways outlined by Piaget, may not be feasible. They may have limited mobility, for example, and/or no peripheral vision, and also be operating at a stage where they are relatively unresponsive to any stimuli, requiring alternative approaches to enabling their learning to be adopted, which arguably need to be mediated by others. Whereas behaviourism, proposed by Skinner, can be found in many classrooms with learners with SLD, for example, through the implementation of ABA for those who are also autistic, its focus arguably tends to be narrow, and revolves around a very precise set of learning goals. Interacting with the research literature on Inclusive Pedagogy, however, and adopting an associated socio-cultural perspective on learning, arguably prompts educators to consider the 'bigger picture' beyond these goals and appreciate the longer-term benefits of building community.

How Do We Develop Teachers for Classrooms with SPMLD Learners?

In addition to debates around curriculum and pedagogy, there are debates relating to how we most effectively train and develop teachers to work with learners with SPMLD. Is a separate specialist route in the teaching profession required for those who intend to go into special schools to work with these learners? Or should all teachers follow more generic routes into teaching? If such generic routes are followed, then what space should be given to considerations around learners with SPMLD within them? Should all programmes of initial teacher training include sessions on SPMLD, for example? Should all trainee teachers be required to spend at least a few days on placement in a school where there are learners with SPMLD? In order to gain qualified teacher status, should a person need to demonstrate some awareness of diverse learning needs? Can professional learning relating to learners with SPMLD be transferred to contexts where there are no SPMLD learners?

Writing in 2015, Mintz & Wyse (2015) emphasised how discussions on preparing teachers to meet the diverse needs of learners have tended to involve a split between 'sociological and psychological positions on SEN' (p. 1166). They associate the writings of Florian and Black-Hawkins (2011) and Black-Hawkins and Florian (2012) on the principle of Inclusive Pedagogy, with ideas within the discipline of Disability Studies, and their origins in the writings of the philosopher Micheal Foucault (1926–1984), on the social construction of categories of difference (pp. 1162–1163). According to Mintz and Wyse, therefore, a commitment to the principle of Inclusive Pedagogy is 'ideological' (p. 1162) and reflects the same 'sociological critique of special education' (p. 1162) that has led to specialist knowledge on conditions such as ADHD historically being absent from initial teacher training programmes (p. 1161). They argue that insights from developmental psychology and neuroscience 'are becoming increasingly difficult to ignore' (p. 1168).

It could be argued, however, that rather than challenge Florian and Black-Hawkins' writings on Inclusive Pedagogy, Mintz and Wyse's position has much in common with it. From my own perspective, Florian and Black-Hawkins do not actually reject specialist insights into SEND in favour of a sociological approach. They argue that inclusive classroom practice requires teachers who can draw upon these insights to 'extend what is ordinarily available to all' and respond to the individual needs of individual pupils. It has also been argued that teacher preparation for inclusive classrooms needs to be interdisciplinary and embrace varied forms of knowledge, rather than reject Sociology. Cornwall (2013) argues that Sociology, Philosophy, History, and Psychology are all important to developing teachers. Through professional learning informed by multidisciplinary approaches, for example, teachers can begin to understand the backgrounds of their learners, establish priorities based on moral values, develop a working knowledge of child development, or of how experiences of trauma can impact wellbeing.

Mintz and Wyse (2015) also explore a perceived separation between 'specialist knowledge' around SEND and 'specialist pedagogies' (p. 1163) for teaching learners with SEND, that is apparent in Lewis and Norwich (2005, cited in Mintz and Wyse, 2015, pp. 1163–1164) publication 'Special Teaching for Special Children?'. In this publication, Lewis and Norwich do not deny that specialist knowledge exists, yet they also assert that the core professional qualities for teaching are universal, and that there is no such thing as specialist pedagogy. For Mintz and Wyse, 'specialist pedagogies' cannot be separated from 'specialist knowledge' (p. 1163). They argue that pedagogy needs to be evidence-informed, otherwise it carries 'the risk of denying groups in society access to the benefits of the scientific approach' (p. 1167). They point out that it is dangerous to reject what Psychology has to offer education, through adopting a solely sociological perspective. However, we may assert that it is possible to simultaneously embrace Psychology and a commitment to the principle of Inclusive Pedagogy and therefore resolve the 'tension' which Mintz and Wyse identify.

Discussion

At first hand, it may appear that school leaders (and others shaping education policy) have very binary choices to make around the education of those with SPMLD, such as those around national curriculum/developmental curriculum, or those around specialist/general teacher training for those aspiring to work in schools where SPMLD learners are present. In my experience, however, there are multiple possibilities beyond any two polarised positions on the schooling of SPMLD learners that may be assumed. As someone who has worked with a vast number of schools, I personally assert that getting things right for learners with SPMLD requires creative and contextualised problem-solving, rather than making a simplistic 'either/or' decision about adopting one approach or another.

One example of creative and contextualised problem-solving, around learners with SPMLD, which I have had the privilege of being part of, has been in relation to initial teacher education, when working at Swiss Cottage School, in London. Swiss Cottage is a specialist setting with a high proportion of SPMLD learners. For years, it has been widely recognised as a centre of excellence and has played an active role in developing educators. In the 2010s, amidst concerns in the sector around recruiting sufficient numbers of teachers to work with SPMLD, Swiss Cottage led the development and delivery of a range of enhanced pathways for trainee teachers, which built their capacity in relation to SEND. We worked with a number of initial teacher training providers to do this, and the University College London Institute of Education (UCL IOE) in particular. For some providers, these enhanced pathways included a one-week placement in a special school, for all those learning to teach, alongside designated days at Swiss Cottage, for focussed sessions. For other providers, it also meant opportunities for extended special school placements and/or participation in a 'SEND Champions' programme, which ran alongside the course for their teaching qualification. Significantly, this innovation around preparing upcoming teachers in relation to SEND, transcended calls for a separate specialist Postgraduate Certificate in Education (SEND) for those wanting to teach SPMLD learners. It also transcended any insistence that issues around inclusion are inherent to any generic teacher education course, without any more dedicated SEND content being required. It did not involve taking a stand on any debates between specialist/general training pathways, and instead shaped something distinct that could be seen as neither (or indeed both!) of these things.

Another example of creative and contextualised problem-solving I have been part of, in relation to learners with SPMLD, is in working with schools that have devised curricula in ways that haven't involved making a binary choice between adopting the national curriculum or subscribing to a more developmental model. Some schools I have worked with, for example, have collapsed national curriculum subjects into broader curriculum areas such as

'People and Planet' through which topics relating to History, Geography, Science, and Religious Education have provided contexts for building independent living skills. Learners may be working on individualised goals related to communication or self-care, but through an activity about Diwali, or a sensory story about Victorian Britain. Although I do not necessarily advocate for an approach such as this (or any particular approach for that matter) I maintain that it can, when undertaken with integrity, be preferable to approaches that are based on a wholesale rejection of traditional school subjects on the national curriculum, as well as preferable to an insistence that the national curriculum is an entitlement of all learners, that should be covered at all costs.

When making strategic decisions about the education of learners with SPMLD, therefore, it may be helpful to be mindful of how there is unlikely to be any universally optimal way of doing things. There are approaches out there, which I would claim are universally 'wrong' (such as insisting on the teaching of phonics to a child working at a developmental level analogous to that of a three-month-old baby). However, I would also claim that there is no single 'right' approach. One special school can organise learners into classes by chronological age and have those with PMLD and those with more moderate learning difficulties in the same teaching group, all following the same curriculum. This may be fine. Another special school may have a class for learners with PMLD, that spans across the 5–14 age range, following a specific PMLD curriculum. This may also be fine.

Whatever the context they are being implemented in, the vast majority of approaches, I have found, have the scope to either be ineffective or ineffective (or ethical or unethical), depending on the circumstances. From my personal perspective, just as the research literature on the principle of Inclusive Pedagogy emphasises that the same action within a classroom can be simultaneously inclusive and exclusive, rather than necessarily either one or the other (Black-Hawkins and Florian, 2012, p. 568), the vast majority of approaches to the education of learners with SPMLD can be simultaneously positive and negative. Some learners in Jonathan Bryan's class may have benefited enormously from that same sensory curriculum that he described as having a detrimental impact on him. Sitting four secondary-aged learners with SLD, around the same table, to collectively create artwork, may successfully develop the social skills of some learners, but undermine levels of engagement in others. Beyond considerations around the best position to take in relation to the questions discussed in this chapter, therefore, it is important for teachers and schools to continually reevaluate what they do as they navigate complex and ambiguous realities. Beyond the abstract notions of best practice, which tend to underpin responses to the questions discussed in this chapter, it is also imperative that teachers and schools continually explore and refer back to the core values that shape the ultimate aims and goals of their work.

From my perspective, one obvious core value, related to the schooling of those with SPMLD, is that of 'authenticity.' I would also go as far as arguing that it is upholding the principle of 'authenticity' itself, rather than any particular curriculum or assessment model, or pedagogy, that will determine the quality and appropriateness of education provision for SPMLD learners. This principle of 'authenticity' can be seen in the strong arguments presented by Imray and Hinchcliffe (2013) for a more developmental curriculum for those with SLD and PMLD. These arguments are largely based on a rejection of inauthentic and tokenistic practices related to the ways in which the national curriculum has been delivered for these learners, which have been discussed above. With this, however, it is important to remember that alternatives to the national curriculum that have been proposed, through a rejection of those inauthentic and tokenistic practices, however great they may seem at first, can themselves lead to practices that are far from authentic. A life-skills-based curriculum designed for learners with SLD can result in learners sequencing cartoon images of the process of cleaning teeth, which has no relation to the way in which they clean their teeth at home. A sensory curriculum, designed for learners with PMLD, can lead to teachers dressing up as characters from stories and effectively ignoring their pupils as they immerse themselves in their role.

The delivery of high-quality education to learners with SPMLD, therefore, requires a culture of active professionalism and reflective practice. Educators need to be granted the agency and autonomy to consider broad questions around what matters for their particular pupils, and what seems to be working for them, in their particular context. When educators become mere consumers or implementers of best practice guidelines (that are based on received wisdom in relation to the questions explored in this chapter), their agency and autonomy risk becoming eroded. In my experience, the consequences of such erosion can be so great, and ultimately have such a negative impact on pupils, that any value that an imposed pedagogical model or approach, however strong its evidence-base, or the arguments for it may be, becomes lost.

Rather than source curricula, assessment systems, and/or teaching methodologies for SPMLD, to 'roll out' or disseminate to classroom staff, school leaders, therefore, should alternatively focus on empowering educators to positively interact with the dilemmas they face. To do this, school leaders need to embrace the inevitable imperfections in policy and practice. A pedagogical approach adopted by a group of teachers, for example, in response to a dilemma around a group of learners, will have its advantages and disadvantages. The approach may also depart from the recommendations of a related research study or how senior leaders within the school may have responded to the dilemma themselves. However, there is an argument that, if the group of teachers is motivated, critical, engaged in dialogues, and enquiry-focussed, then none of this matters. Rather than finding definitive answers to the questions discussed in this chapter, the role of school leaders, researchers, and those involved in teacher education, it could be claimed, is to keep dialogues in relation to these questions alive. To do this, investment needs to be made in dilemma-based approaches to the professional learning of those working with learners with SPMLD, which are explored within the final chapter of this book.

References

Alexander, R. (2004). Still no pedagogy? Principle, pragmatism and compliance in primary education. *Cambridge Journal of Education*, *34*(1). https://doi.org/10.1080/0305764042000183106

American Psychological Association. (2017). *APA Policy: Applied Behavior Analysis*. Retrieved from: http://www.apa.org/about/policy/applied-behavior-analysis

Black-Hawkins, K., & Florian, L. (2012). Classroom teachers craft knowledge of their inclusive practice. *Teachers and Teaching: Theory and Practice*, *18*(5). https://doi.org/10.1080/13540602.2012.709732

Bryan, J. (2018). *Eye Can Write: A Memoir of a Child's Silent Soul Emerging*. London, England: Bonnier (Lagom).

Byers, R., & Lawson, H. (2015). Priorities, products and process: Developments in providing a curriculum for learners with SLD/PMLD. In P. Lacey, R. Ashdown, P. Jones, H. Lawson, & M. Pipe (Eds.), *The Routledge Companion to Severe, Profound and Multiple Learning Difficulties*. London, England: Routledge.

Colley, A. (2020). To what extent have learners with severe, profound and multiple learning difficulties been excluded from the policy and practice of inclusive education? *International Journal of Inclusive Education*, *24*(7). https://doi.org/10.1080/13603116.2018.1483437

Cornwall, J. (2013). What makes an inclusive teacher? Can fish climb trees? Mapping the European agency profile of inclusive teachers to the english system. *FORUM*, *55*(1). https://doi.org/10.2304/forum.2013.55.1.103

Daniels, H. (2009). Vygotsky and inclusion. In P. Hick, R. Kershner, & P. Farrell (Eds.), *Psychology for Inclusive Education: New Directions in Theory and Practice* (pp. 24–38). Routledge. https://doi.org/10.4324/9780203891476-9

Davies, G. (2025, 6th May). *Attention Autism*. Retrieved from https://ginadavies.co.uk/attention-autism/

EADSNE. (2012). TE I Teacher Education for Inclusion Teacher Education for Inclusion *Profile of Inclusive Teachers*. Retrieved from https://www.european-agency.org/resources/publications/teacher-education-inclusion-profile-inclusive-teachers

Florian, L., & Black-Hawkins, K. (2011). Exploring inclusive pedagogy. *British Educational Research Journal*, *37*(5), 813–828. https://doi.org/10.1080/01411926.2010.501096

Florian, L., & Rouse, M. (2010). Teachers' professional learning and inclusive practice. In *Confronting Obstacles to Inclusion: International Responses to Developing Inclusive Education*. London: Routledge.

Imray, P., & Hinchcliffe, V. (2012). Not fit for purpose: A call for separate and distinct pedagogies as part of a national framework for those with severe and profound learning difficulties. *Support for Learning*, *27*(4). https://doi.org/10.1111/1467-9604.12002

Imray, P., & Hinchcliffe, V. (2013). Curricula for teaching children and young people with severe or profound and multiple learning difficulties: Practical strategies for educational professionals. In *Curricula for Teaching Children and Young People with Severe or Profound and Multiple Learning Difficulties: Practical Strategies for Educational Professionals*. https://doi.org/10.4324/9781315883298

Jones, P., & Lawson, H. (2015). Insights into teacher learning about pedagogy from an international group of teachers of students with severe intellectual disabilities. *European Journal of Special Needs Education*, *30*(3). https://doi.org/10.1080/08856257.2015.1023000

Lewis, A., & Norwich, B. (2007). Special teaching for special children? Pedagogies for inclusion. *Educational and Child Psychology*, *24*(3).

Mintz, J., & Wyse, D. (2015). Inclusive pedagogy and knowledge in special education: Addressing the tension. *International Journal of Inclusive Education*, *19*(11). https://doi.org/10.1080/13603116.2015.1044203

Noddings, N. (2005). Identifying and responding to needs in education. *Cambridge Journal of Education*, *35*(2), 147–159. https://doi.org/10.1080/03057640500146757

Noddings, N. (2013). *Caring: A Relational Approach to Ethics and Moral Education* (2nd ed.). University of California Press.

Rix, J., & Sheehy, K. (2014). Nothing special: The everyday pedagogy of teaching. In *The SAGE Handbook of Special Education: Two Volume Set, Second Edition*. https://doi.org/10.4135/9781446282236.n29

Slee, R. (2013). How do we make inclusive education happen when exclusion is a political predisposition? In *International Journal of Inclusive Education*. *17(8)* https://doi.org/10.1080/13603116.2011.602534

Spratt, J., & Florian, L. (2014). Developing and using a framework for gauging the use of inclusive pedagogy by new and experienced teachers. *International Perspectives on Inclusive Education*, *3*. https://doi.org/10.1108/S1479-363620140000003029

Spratt, J., & Florian, L. (2015). Inclusive pedagogy: From learning to action. Supporting each individual in the context of "everybody". *Teaching and Teacher Education*, *49*. https://doi.org/10.1016/j.tate.2015.03.006

Stewart, C., & Walker-Gleaves, C. (2020). A narrative exploration of how curricula for children with profound and multiple learning difficulties shape and are shaped by the practices of their teachers. *British Journal of Special Education*, *47*(3), 350–375. https://doi.org/10.1111/1467-8578.12313

Teach Us Too. (2025, 10 May). *Teach Us Too: Promoting an education system where all children are taught literacy regardless of their label*. Retrieved from https://www.teachustoo.org.uk

West-Burnham, J., & Coates, M. (2005). *Personalizing Learning: Transforming Education for Every Child*. London, England: Bloomsbury.

Zhou, K., Liu, X., Li, S., Zhang, Y., An, R., & Ma, S. (2024). The use of Treatment and Education of Autistic and Related Communication Handicapped Children in schools to improve the ability of children with autism to complete tasks independently: A single-case meta-analysis. *Child: Care, Health and Development*, *50*(2) https://doi.org/10.1111/cch.13234

Part 2

'Dilemma stories' from teachers of SPMLD learners

Chapter 4

Should I be having this conversation about death?

As a secondary teacher within a local authority with only two small special schools, Polly works with young people with a range of complex needs. This includes pupils with SLD, working at a developmental level often associated with being of preschool age. These learners may need support finding classrooms that they go to every day. Others may also need support with personal care and/or continence issues. Their school week, therefore, typically includes allocated hours with a one-to-one support assistant, as well as allocated time to be removed from the mainstream classroom, to be taught in a small group, by the Deputy Special Educational Needs Coordinator (DSENCO). In these small groups, these learners spend time revisiting phonics and engaging in tasks to support reading. They also complete learning activities related to early Mathematics, such as counting and solving simple addition problems.

The subject which Polly teaches at her school, Religious Education (RE), had been taught in mixed attainment groups for as long as any of her departmental colleagues could remember. This meant that classes had always been exceptionally diverse, including individuals who were excelling academically, as well as individuals with SLD, who were not removed from lessons in this subject. This inclusion of learners with SLD posed a challenge for Polly, who worried about the appropriateness of aspects of the RE curriculum for some of her older learners, who did not seem developmentally ready to engage with complex debates related to topics such as terrorism or euthanasia.

When teaching a unit on 'Death,' Polly also wondered whether-or-not she was capable enough to answer any questions raised by learners with SLD and find the right words to support them through any anxieties that may arise. In relation to this, she also started to question the boundaries of her role as an RE teacher. Was it her place to provide emotional support to these learners, without having specialist training first, to develop a specialist skill set? Should she just not focus instead on providing a straightforward differentiated task for them to complete (such as colouring a picture of a Mexican Day of the Dead sugar skull), which, whilst being broadly based on the topic, would enable her to, in reality, circumnavigate the sensitive issues associated with it?

DOI: 10.4324/9781003540106-7

> Teaching 'Death' is something that I've really grappled with in relation to some of our learners with SEND. Quite often I think … Should I be even including some of this stuff in their learning? Or should I miss it out entirely? Is it too difficult? Is it too difficult to talk to a SEND student with complex needs about death? Is it too difficult to talk about some of those emotional realities?' One of our RE units is 'Islam and Equality' and we cover things like extremism. And I think to myself; Should we be? Is this too much?

As an RE teacher, however, Polly believes that it is an entitlement of all children and young people to have opportunities to interact with topics which are central to the human experience. She sees this as ultimately fundamental to their safety and wellbeing, therefore placing a moral imperative upon schools to address the associated challenges head-on, rather than avoid them.

> You question whether the curriculum is appropriate, but then I think the reality is, a lot of it **is** appropriate. Without that learning, there's a safeguarding issue with the students. If I don't teach a student about death, it doesn't mean that death isn't going to happen to them.

When teaching the unit on 'Death,' Polly found herself in a particularly difficult situation involving 'Hafsa,' a young person with identified SLD, who also had Downs Syndrome and complex behavioural issues. At the age of 14, Hafsa had no awareness of the reality that life eventually reaches an end. This meant that, when her Grandad died a few weeks earlier, she had no understanding of what was happening:

> I remember the conversation. It was a really difficult one. She said 'Oh, my Grandad's died. Does that mean he's not coming back?' and I said 'yes, that is what it means. Your grandad won't be coming back'. I also had to be mindful of religious beliefs because a lot of our students believe in heaven, so it was really difficult. I had to say 'Your Grandad won't come back **to Earth**. He won't come back to live with us. He won't come back to live with you. He's been in hospital. He was sick and he didn't get better and that can happen sometimes'. I remember feeling really out of my depth. I was unsure over whether or not I should be having those conversations.

Polly's story, about teaching the topic of 'Death' to Hafsa, within a mixed attainment teaching group, raises multiple important questions around the inclusion of learners with SLD in mainstream secondary schools. We could ask, for example, whether it is feasible to expect Polly to divide her time between supporting Hafsa and teaching the other students in her class, who were all preparing for their GCSE examinations.

To enable Hafsa to process the loss of her Grandad, Polly found herself having 'three conversations, on three separate weeks, to help her to understand'. It could be argued, from a utilitarian perspective, which associates ethical decision-making with the anticipated benefits to the majority, that this was not an appropriate use of Polly's time. Although it may have been beneficial to Hafsa herself, this argument might go, it was possibly detrimental to the majority of learners, who were being deprived of teaching from Polly, whilst those three conversations were happening. Also, from a utilitarian perspective, it could be argued that the policy of inclusion, within the local authority where the school resides, through which those with SLD are placed in mainstream schools, is ultimately unethical. It is a policy, it might be claimed, which doesn't lead to the greatest good, to the greatest number of people. Instead (so the argument goes) it makes it harder for the majority of children and young people within the local authority, (many of whom will come from deprived backgrounds) to learn, attain high grades, and eventually achieve social mobility.

There are various assumptions behind utilitarian arguments against educating Hafsa and other young people with SLD in mainstream school settings; however, these assumptions are controversial. For example, the assumption of a direct causal thread between Polly taking the time to have three separate conversations with this learner and the lowering of the attainment of the other learners in the class is problematic. Is it not, in fact, beneficial for all learners to have opportunities for independent and/or collaborative enquiry within an RE lesson that reduces their dependency on the teacher? If such opportunities are planned carefully and are structured, do they not ultimately lead to improved learning outcomes, which would be difficult to reach if the pedagogical focus were always on direct instruction? Is the way in which Polly organises learning within her classroom, to enable her to target support where it is most needed, actually a good thing, rather than an awkward compromise between the needs of the majority and the needs of the minority, that are alleged to be competing?

In writing about inclusive pedagogical classroom practice, Spratt and Florian (2015) emphasise the importance of getting the social dynamics within the classroom right, as a basis for deep learning. It is through establishing such social dynamics, it could be argued, that the inclusion of Hafsa in Polly's RE lessons becomes more manageable and sustainable. Rather than planning for 'some' and 'most' learners, inclusive pedagogical practice involves planning for 'everybody' (Spratt and Florian, 2015). This means a departure from setting a range of tasks, at different levels of difficulty within a classroom, and away from dispensing them to different perceived ability groups. Instead, teachers focus on 'getting the micro-culture of the classroom right, to enable all children to thrive' (Spratt and Florian, 2015, p. 90). One example of this, given by Spratt and Florian, is in the practice of 'Mary' (Spratt and Florian, 2015, p. 93). In an observed lesson on 'a' words and 'an' words, Mary had a carousel of four activities in place, for small groups of learners to rotate around. One activity, for example, required children to work together to sort a deck of word-cards into two piles. Another activity involved children writing a list of 'a' and 'an' words onto a large sheet of paper. The lesson, therefore, offered opportunities for cooperative learning and represented a movement away from separate teacher-led differentiated activities, based on notions of ability. Rather than being ability-based, the small groups of children working together in Mary's lesson had varying levels of prior attainment and were learning in ways consistent with the socio-cultural and/or Vygotskian approaches outlined by Daniels (2009). Although the difference between 'a' and 'an' words is arguably meaningless to those who do not have sufficient levels of literacy to recognise their name in print, these activities may have had secondary benefits that they could access (such as using fine motor skills to glue down the cards). Although not without their obvious challenges, similar small group activities in a RE lesson on 'Death,' such as discussing artistic representations of heaven and hell on laminated cards, or sorting quotes from sacred texts on a large Venn diagram, may have effectively extended the critical thinking of many pupils, whilst either facilitating Hafsa's inclusion and/or freeing up Polly to spend time with her.

The utilitarian assumption that the needs of the majority of learners outweigh Hafsa's individual human rights can also be questioned. This is an assumption that is based on an insistence that Hafsa is only one person, and that improved outcomes for her alone have less value than improved outcomes for two, three, six, or ten young people. Such an assumption disregards considerations around the *extent* to which outcomes are improved for multiple people within a situation, and the extent to which they are improved for the individual. Hypothetically, a decision by Polly to ignore Hafsa and leave her to colour in a picture without any interaction may benefit at least five other young people in her class by giving her time to go over to them, to talk with them about the shortcuts they could use when undertaking exam revision. Although five is a greater number than one, however, such a decision would essentially be depriving Hafsa of various fundamental entitlements that are enshrined in the various articles within the United Nations Convention on the Rights of the Child (UNICEF, UK, 2025). By merely completing a colouring activity in the corner of the classroom, for example, Hafsa would arguably not be accessing her right to an education (Article 28). By not having her difficulties around comprehending the concept of death addressed by Polly, and/or the other adults around her, Hafsa is also not accessing her right to live a full, decent, and dignified life, as a disabled child, with the support in place to enable full participation in her community (Article 23). The other five learners in the class, however, who Polly may be talking to, if she was not spending time with Hafsa, are already accessing these rights. Rather than approach the question of whether-or-not she should be having the conversation with Hafsa about death from a utilitarian perspective, therefore, it could be argued that Polly should instead be focussing on ensuring that each individual in their class is having their essential needs met. If any individual doesn't have these needs met, then that is a higher priority than that of maximising the happiness of the others.

As an alternative to utilitarianism, the Capability Approach, associated with the writings of Amartya Sen (2001) and Martha Nussbaum (2011) serves as a framework for exploring Polly's dilemma, which is more appreciative of the nuances around the varying extent to which our actions impact people differently. Rather than being consequentialist, and based on the anticipated outcomes of our actions, the Capability Approach (also referred to as the Capabilities Approach) has a basis in the Kantian notion that human beings are not a means-to-an-end but an 'end' themselves (Sen, 2001, p. 157). Ethical conduct, therefore, is in what enables human flourishing at an individual level, rather than in the projected long-term overall outcomes that this is expected to lead to. Under the Capability Approach, therefore, a key purpose of education is to enable those who access it to thrive. Young people in schools, therefore, it could be argued with reference to the approach, should not merely be viewed as vehicles for equipping a growing economy with a skilled workforce, to enable a country to increase its overall Gross Domestic Product (GDP). Instead, education should centre around the young people themselves and their wellbeing.

In her writings on the Capabilities Approach, Nussbaum (2011) responds to the question 'What is each person able to do and to be?' by outlining a set of Ten Central Capabilities. This is a list of ten freedoms, or entitlements, which human beings need to have access to, to live a minimally flourishing life. Nussbaum's list of 'Ten Central Capabilities' includes 'life,' 'bodily health,' 'bodily integrity,' 'senses, imagination, and thought,' 'emotions,' 'practical reason,' 'affiliation,' 'other species,' 'play,' and 'control over one's environment' (Nussbaum, 2011, pp. 33–34). It is also noteworthy that Nussbaum (2011) emphasised that the purpose of the Capabilities Approach is not for all citizens of the world to access each of these ten capabilities equally. The point, rather, is for all people to reach a minimum threshold of acceptability for each of the Ten Central Capabilities and also to ultimately realise each one to the maximum degree possible. For Polly, this would mean prioritising Hafsa, at times when it becomes apparent that she has not reached this minimum threshold.

One of the ten central capabilities outlined by Nussbaum, for example, is 'control over one's environment' (p. 34). This includes having political control, for example, through participation in democratic processes. It also includes material control, through having employment rights or being entitled to own property. It is ultimately highly likely that, as adults in the future, some of the learners in Polly's RE class will end up having greater control over their environment than others. Some may go on to be politicians, playing a key role in the decisions that affect them. Others may find themselves working under contracts with controversial restrictions. The extent to which different individuals from Polly's class have control over their environment is also likely to vary throughout their life course. Some may spend time in prison, where they are unable to vote and have much less control over what is happening around them than at other points in their lives. Others may spend a proportion of their career running a successful business, which has an influential voice in the community, before having to stop upon being incapacitated due to terminal illness. As an individual with SLD, Hafsa is likely to need considerable support from others to have any significant control over her environment. Although professional advocates may be appointed, at various stages in her life, to elicit her views on the various decisions that affect her (e.g., around education beyond school, or social care), these decisions will reflect local and national policies and infrastructure that she will be unlikely to have played a meaningful role in shaping. A recognition of this emphasises the value of learning activities for Hafsa, which enable more effective communication and interaction with others, so that the capability of 'having control over one's environment' can be enjoyed at some level. When teaching the unit on 'Death,' Polly found herself working with Hafsa to repurpose a shoe box into a casket of memories about her Grandad. This included photographs, significant objects, and decorations in his favourite colours. Rather than be something which Polly had initially planned to do with Hafsa, it was something that was iteratively planned, in response to the needs that she was eliciting from this learner through her teaching. Whereas Hafsa may not understand the mechanics of the school council or be in a position to write a letter to her local member of parliament, she was being enabled to ensure that her learning environment, in that moment, reflected her feelings and aspirations.

With this in mind, Polly's work with Hafsa, when teaching this unit on 'Death,' also highlights possible synergy between inclusive pedagogical decision-making that is aligned with the Capability Approach, and the principle proposed by Noddings (2005) that teachers think beyond the 'inferred' needs of learners, to work with their 'expressed needs' (p. 148). In completing the 'shoebox task' with Hafsa, Polly was responding to such 'expressed' needs, rather than issuing a differentiated activity to Hafsa and other learners with the class with low prior attainment, around the generic label of 'Special Educational Needs.'

To some extent, Polly's work with Hafsa also aligns with the principle of Inclusive Pedagogy, associated with the writings of Lani Florian and others (e.g., Black-Hawkins and Florian, 2012; Spratt and Florian, 2014; Florian, 2015b). Across the literature in this area, the relationship between inclusive pedagogical practice and the professional Craft knowledge of teachers is emphasised (e.g., Florian and Black-Hawkins, 2011; Black-Hawkins and Florian, 2012; Florian and Graham, 2014). Craft knowledge is tacit knowledge or 'practical wisdom' (Florian and Beaton 2018, p.873) that can be used by teachers to discern the most appropriate course of action to take in a particular situation. In deciding to complete the shoebox task with Hafsa, Polly was exercising her own 'Craft knowledge' to reach the conclusion that this would be the most valuable use of curriculum time with her.

Central to the definition of Inclusive Pedagogy, however, is the suggestion that teachers focus on 'extending what is ordinarily available for all learners' rather than on offering something additional for 'some' (Black-Hawkins and Florian 2012, p. 575). Rather than do this, Polly in fact did find herself doing something entirely different with Hafsa, from what the rest of the class were doing. This story, therefore, about teaching the unit on 'Death,' arguably suggests that the extent to which teachers can feasibly extend 'what is ordinarily available' to all pupils has boundaries. Rather than construct narrative answers to GCSE questions about religious views on the afterlife, it was more purposeful for Hafsa to work on creating a casket of memories about her Grandad in Polly's RE lessons.

Through its suggestion that teachers focus on 'extending what is ordinarily available to all' pupils, the principle of Inclusive Pedagogy, therefore, has been presented as a response to 'the dilemma of difference' (e.g., Florian, 2010, p. 62), which has long dominated discussions around decision-making processes relating to children and young people with special educational needs and disabilities (e.g., Norwich 2008). The 'dilemma of difference' is the dilemma which arises out of a simultaneous desire to respond to individual needs in individualised ways, and a desire to not represent these individuals as subnormal 'others,' who deviate from what is perceived to be typical.

Through implementing an Inclusive Pedagogy and 'extending what is ordinarily available to all' it has been argued teachers can enhance access to core teaching and learning activities, reducing the need to provide a less challenging task to learners who are perceived to be low ability, thus avoiding this 'othering' (e.g., Spratt and Florian, 2015). An RE teacher, for example, might ask learners to select from a choice of images and quotes, the card that they 'like the best' or that best represents their views on the afterlife, thereby providing challenge for learners aiming for high GCSE grades, alongside opportunities for participation for many of those with significant learning difficulties. Such an activity, however, may not have been beneficial to Hafsa. Due to her comprehension difficulties, when asked to select a card, she may have struggled to understand what was being asked of her. Rather than make an authentic choice, when selecting a card, and meaningfully engaging with learning outcomes for the lesson, she may have ended up pointing at any random one (imitating what she had seen the other young people do) in order to merely survive the feeling of discomfort she was experiencing throughout the lesson. Under these circumstances, 'extending what was already available to all' learners may not have in fact strengthened Hafsa's participation. Instead, it would have merely given a superficial appearance of inclusive practice, which, for the teacher, Polly, would have been highly performative.

In Polly's story, therefore, she does not seem to be grappling with the 'dilemma of difference.' Within a classroom culture which embraces diversity, it did not feel compromising for her to offer something different to an individual learner, if their 'expressed needs' (Noddings, 2005, p. 148) were being addressed through this. Instead, Polly seemed to be navigating a 'Dilemma of Possibility' through which she questioned whether-or not responding to these 'expressed needs' was an appropriate thing for her to do, in relation to her role as a subject teacher. In her story, Polly wondered whether-or-not she was equipped with the requisite set of skills for supporting a young person with SLD to process bereavement. She wondered whether-or-not she 'should' be having the conversation with her about death, or whether-or-not this should be somebody else's job. Ultimately, however, Polly concluded that the elusive expertise in SLD, which she was initially imagining, did not in fact exist (or, at least, was not available to Hafsa by anybody else within the school). It was therefore down to Polly, as the professional in this encounter with the young person, to draw upon her own resources to support her. If Polly was not herself going to step up and support this learner, then who else would do it?

Although Polly's practice is not based on 'extending what is ordinarily available to all,' there are in fact parallels between overcoming the 'dilemma of possibility' around teaching learners with complex needs, and writings on the implementation of Inclusive Pedagogy. The Inclusive Pedagogical Approach in Action (IPAA) framework was developed in 2014 (Florian, 2014; Spratt and Florian, 2014; Florian, 2015a) as a resource for capturing, articulating, and evaluating inclusive pedagogical practice. Within this framework, the association between Inclusive Pedagogy and the belief that all teachers are capable of teaching all learners is highlighted. With this in mind, it is arguably not necessarily doing something different with Hafsa in the mainstream classroom that stigmatises or 'others' her. It is the view that she is somehow distinct, or even alien, from other young people, and that it is not 'possible' for anyone to work with her, without very specific expertise for doing so.

Polly ended up having several conversations with Hafsa's Mum, who was overwhelmingly positive about the impact that creating the casket of memories had on the wellbeing and development of her daughter. This eliminated many of Polly's doubts around being capable enough to teach learners with SLD. It also affirmed her decision to persist in having the difficult conversation about death with Hafsa, rather than avoid it. Although Polly had never attended a specialist course on severe learning difficulties and often felt that she was lacking in requisite specialist knowledge for teaching learners with complex profiles such as Hafsa, she had more tacit knowledge in this situation to draw upon, as well as her core humanity.

References

Daniels, H. (2009). Vygotsky and inclusion. In P. Hick, R. Kershner, & P. Farrell (Eds.), *Psychology for Inclusive Education: New Directions in Theory and Practice* (pp. 24–38). London, England: Routledge. https://doi.org/10.4324/9780203891476-9

Black-Hawkins, K., & Florian, L. (2012). Classroom teachers craft knowledge of their inclusive practice. *Teachers and Teaching: Theory and Practice*, 18(5). https://doi.org/10.1080/13540602.2012.709732

Florian, L. (2010). The concept of inclusive pedagogy. In *Transforming the Role of the SENCO: Achieving the National Award for SEN Coordination* (Vol. 1, pp. 62–70). Maidenhead: Open University Press.

Florian, L. (2014). What counts as evidence of inclusive education? *European Journal of Special Needs Education*, *29*(3). https://doi.org/10.1080/08856257.2014.933551

Florian, L. (2015a). Conceptualising inclusive pedagogy: The inclusive pedagogical approach in action. In J. M. Deppeler, T. Loreman, R. Smith, & L. Florian (Eds.), *International Perspectives on Inclusive Education* (Vol. 7). Bingley, England: Emerald. https://doi.org/10.1108/S1479-363620150000007001

Florian L. (2015b). Inclusive pedagogy: A transformative approach to individual differences but can it help reduce educational inequalities? *Scottish Educational Review*, *47*(1). https://doi.org/10.1163/27730840-04701003

Florian, L., & Beaton, M. (2018). Inclusive pedagogy in action: Getting it right for every child. *International Journal of Inclusive Education*, *22*(8). https://doi.org/10.1080/13603116.2017.1412513

Florian, L., & Black-Hawkins, K. (2011). Exploring inclusive pedagogy. *British Educational Research Journal*, *37*(5), 813–828. https://doi.org/10.1080/01411926.2010.501096

Florian, L., & Graham, A. (2014). Can an expanded interpretation of *phronesis* support teacher professional development for inclusion? *Cambridge Journal of Education*, *44*(4), 465–478. https://doi.org/10.1080/0305764X.2014.960910

Noddings, N. (2005). Identifying and responding to needs in education. *Cambridge Journal of Education*, *35*(2), 147–159. https://doi.org/10.1080/03057640500146757

Norwich, B. (2008). Dilemmas of difference, inclusion and disability: International perspectives on placement. *European Journal of Special Needs Education*, *23*(4). https://doi.org/10.1080/08856250802387166

Nussbaum, M. (2011). *Creating Capabilities: The Human Development Approach*. Cambridge, Massachusetts: The Belknap Press of Harvard University Press.

Sen, A. (2001). *Development as Freedom*. Oxford, England: Oxford University Press.

Spratt, J., & Florian, L. (2014). Developing and using a framework for gauging the use of inclusive pedagogy by new and experienced teachers. *International Perspectives on Inclusive Education*, *3*. https://doi.org/10.1108/S1479-363620140000003029

Spratt, J., & Florian, L. (2015). Inclusive pedagogy: From learning to action. Supporting each individual in the context of "everybody". *Teaching and Teacher Education*, *49*. https://doi.org/10.1016/j.tate.2015.03.006

UNICEF, U. (2025, 6th May). *How we protect children's rights: With the UN Convention on the Rights of the Child*. Available at: https://www.unicef.org.uk/what-we-do/un-convention-child-rights/

Chapter 5

How do we, as a team, develop an effective behavioural strategy for a learner with autism?

The experience of Carlos, in his story, of leading a team supporting a young person in crisis within a special school, is likely to resonate with many educators working in this sector. Carlos is a lead practitioner with responsibility for learner behaviour. When 'James,' therefore, a 13-year-old learner with autism and severe learning difficulties, starts presenting with various distressed and disruptive behaviours, Carlos has a key role to play in guiding discussions and in exploring possible strategies with colleagues.

As well as Carlos, the core team working with James included his class teacher, the two teaching assistants assigned to his class, and a behaviour mentor who worked across the entire school. It also included James' Mum and had occasional input from a speech and language therapist, who, despite having a huge case load, was able to devote some working hours to what had become an acute situation. When James' distressed behaviours peaked, he would spend much of the school day outside of the classroom, often ripping down corridor displays, upturning bins, and dangerously throwing any objects that got in his way, including chairs. James would also self-harm by punching walls and scratching himself. He would therefore often need to be physically restrained and required two adults to be with him each time he wandered out of class, meaning that the others in the teaching group, within which there were young people with other complex behavioural issues, were being left alone with only one individual staff member.

Carlos and his colleagues trialled a number of strategies with James. Some of these strategies were effective straight away. Others needed to be refined, and some needed to be abandoned altogether, because they were found not to have any positive impact. To support decision-making around what strategies to use, and how and when they might be implemented, the team 'scrutinised behaviour data' and 'discussed what the data could mean.' Through this, for example, they were able to identify possible triggers, which may have led to James' angry outbursts, as well as times within the school day that seemed to be particularly distressing for him. The team could also monitor the impact that any new or adapted approaches seemed to be having. Were these approaches apparently leading to a reduction in the frequency of incidents?

Were they enabling him to stay within his classroom for longer periods of time, and engage with learning?

Through their practice and approach to working with James, Carlos and his team were therefore engaging in the 'Dilemma of What's Working?' This is one of the dilemmas within the typology of 'Four Dilemmas for Inclusive Practice' that was arrived at through the analysis of Carlos' study, alongside other stories shared by other teachers with an interest in inclusive practice, as part of a wider research study.

The 'Dilemma of What's Working?' is a dilemma which involves asking questions around whether-or-not to persist with particular practices, based on interim assessments around their efficacy and impact. It involves considerations around whether-or-not approaches seem to be 'working,' in relation to a particular issue or situation.

For Carlos and his colleagues, navigating the 'Dilemma of What's Working?' involved five-minute team debriefing sessions after the end of each school day, and daily phone calls with James' Mum, as well as weekly meetings between Carlos and James' class teacher. This enabled them to reach difficult decisions around whether-or-not to continue or discontinue with a particular approach or strategy. In reaching these decisions, the team needed to navigate possible ambiguities, to reach valid interpretations of what was going on for James, through processes of reflection and evaluation. Although today was a better day (they asked themselves, for example), were the 'break' cards he was issued with, to enable him to request time out of class, helpful, or were they making things harder?

Alongside this 'Dilemma of What's Working,' therefore, Carlos and his team were also engaging in what could be referred to as a 'Dilemma of Looking?', which is another dilemma underpinning the 'Four Dilemmas of Inclusive Practice,' which was reached through the analysis of the teachers' stories. This 'Dilemma of Looking?' involves observing the responses of pupils and/or dynamics within teaching groups and striving to make sense out of what can be 'seen' (or elicited through other senses such as hearing). Through this Dilemma of 'Looking,' practitioners inevitably grapple with their professional perceptions, values, and attitudes, as well as their conceptions of where truth is located within a school or classroom. Are we seeing an overall reduction in James' distress through him being in his classroom for a greater proportion of the school day, or are we witnessing that he is, in fact, more anxious internally, and likely to cause even greater harm to himself, through the way in which he is silently, and continually, pinching his body?

The distinction between the question 'What Works?' in relation to interventions in education settings, and the question 'What's Working?' is a fundamental one. For years, the term 'What Works?' has underpinned dominant discourses related to effectiveness in education. It is a term, for example, which underpins the work of the Education Endowment Foundation (2025), who work to establish and disseminate evidence-based approaches for improving the educational outcomes of children and young people. Typically, these evidence-based approaches are validated through the results of randomised control trials, through which an approach, such as the use of a particular programme for teaching early literacy, is used with an 'intervention' group. The outcomes for this 'intervention' group are then compared to those of a control group, who have not had access to this same approach. Through this, it can be claimed that we can evaluate whether-or-not the approach 'works' and whether-or-not its use can be scaled up, to enable a greater number of children and young people to benefit from it.

Whereas the question 'What Works?' has value, in Carlos' story about supporting James, the alternative question 'What's Working?' is arguably much more meaningful. The phrase 'What's Working?' emphasises the provisional nature of success in relation to interventions and approaches. The phrase 'What's Working?' suggests that a strategy or approach that is evidently working in one moment will not necessarily do so in the next.

It could be easily argued that utilitarian decision-making, based on the principle that our actions should lead to the greatest good, for the greatest number of people, tends to have coherence with the phrase 'What Work's?'. In common with utilitarianism, the phrase 'What works?' could be charged with being based on simplistic assumptions of a direct causal thread between action and outcome. Whereas a focus on 'What works?' prompts teachers to passively make decisions on the basis of abstract research evidence, the phrase 'What's Working,' whilst not disregarding this research evidence, requires teachers to be active thinkers, exploring the ambiguous and multi-dimensional outcomes of the choices they make, in relation to their own learners.

Across special education globally, a wide array of specialist pedagogies are available to teachers and schools, which also claim to be evidence-based and to 'work.' For example, Applied Behavioural Analysis (ABA) is based on the behaviourist psychology of Skinner (1938 in Foran et al., 2015) and typically involves a process of conditioning through a system of sanctions and rewards with autistic learners. It is an approach that was available to Carlos and his team to use with James to reinforce desirable behaviours and ensure his compliance. A rich evidence base certainly exists to support any rationale, which Carlos might give to James' Mum in the daily telephone conversations for using it. Through randomised control trials, for example, ABA has been found to lead to higher IQ and a decrease in challenging behaviour (e.g., Foran et al., 2015). Carlos and his colleagues, however, had questions about the sustainability and long-term impact of ABA approaches. Arguments made against the use of ABA in special education settings include that it has been associated with post-traumatic stress disorder (e.g., Kupferstein, 2018) and that its focus on behaviour modification in the short term, undermines the capacity for education to develop skills such as those related to self-advocacy and communication, which would be more beneficial to James in the long term. It could alternatively be argued, however, that given the critical and dangerous nature of the situation, it was appropriate to focus on the short-term goal of preventing harm to James or any other member of the school community. From a pragmatic perspective, ABA could be seen as a means to avoid making a bad situation worse, even though its use arguably departs from the ideal.

Whether-or-not a decision is made to use ABA with James, the notion of 'The Dilemma of What's Working?' positions Carlos and members of his team as active professionals with the capacity to adopt a critical perspective on research evidence, and also reflect on, and analyse, practice. Arguably, the term 'What Works?' does not do this as effectively.

By thinking beyond 'What works?' and engaging with the 'Dilemma of What's Working?', Carlos and his team are applying their more tacit professional 'Craft knowledge,' alongside received notions of good practice, that have emerged out of research. One strategy which they used with James, for example, was a printed visual timetable of his school day to take home, to support him to have conversations with his Mum. The effectiveness of visual timetables for learners with autism has been found in multiple randomised control trials (e.g., Dettmer et al., 2000; Pierce et al., 2013). However, it was the exercise of the more tacit Craft knowledge of Carlos and the members of the team, which enabled them to develop an approach to using visual timetables in a particular way, to support James with his particular difficulties. One source of James' distress in school, they had established, was his perception that his entire day had 'gone wrong' once any minor incident had occurred, which led to his behaviour falling short of perfection. He would worry about his parents receiving the news that he had had a 'bad day' as he didn't want to disappoint them. Having a visual timetable to take home, therefore, enabled him to have a more nuanced dialogue with his Mum about what had gone well and what could have gone better. In time, this led to him no longer being so fatalistic when confronted with a relatively small issue or problem, and to understand that there was time to turn things around if his day had started off badly.

Arguably, an over-emphasis on 'What works?' in education can, in fact, undermine outcomes for some pupils. Writing in 2015, Jones & Lawson (2015) describe how, in the US State of Florida, evidence-based pedagogies have led to the proliferation of commercial packages relating to specialist SEND pedagogies, which teachers are 'obliged to take on' (p. 395). Teaching, therefore, becomes about the passive implantation of what is deemed to 'work,' rather than about actively engaging with the unique challenges that unique children and young people bring to the classroom. If teachers are merely using resources and methods that are deemed to 'work,' teaching becomes no longer an interactive process. According to Wrigley, this is actually also the case in medicine. He cites Greenhalgh et al. (2014, cited in Wrigley, 2018) who point out that doctors often need to go against what the evidence is suggesting, because of the unique health profiles of individual patients. According to Greenhalgh et al, a patient attending a GP surgery is unlikely to emulate those selected to be part of an RCT from which those with comorbidities (other coexisting conditions) would have most likely been screened out, so as not to 'distort' the results. Similarly, an educational intervention found to 'work,' through an RCT with particular groups of young people, may not actually be effective with the groups of young people being taught by a particular teacher reading a summary of this RCT. In relation to Carlos' story, and its location within a special school, it is also noteworthy that many RCTs exploring the use of specialist pedagogies for learners with SEND, assume that all pupils with the same label learn in the same way. Setting up 'intervention' and 'control' groups involving only pupils with Down Syndrome (e.g., to test a pedagogy designed for pupils with this diagnosis) would be failing to recognise the heterogeneity of this population, and the overwhelming likelihood that the two groups would be impossible to compare to one another. Some learners with Down Syndrome sit GCSE examinations, whereas others have PMLD. Beyond drawing upon the results of such RCTs, to plan education provision for learners with Down Syndrome, therefore, teachers and schools need to conduct formative assessments, exercise Craft knowledge, and recognise that learners are so much more than a label.

This argument, that individuals are much more than their primary need, diagnosis, or label, raises important considerations about the debates between person-first and identity-first language, in relation to learners such as the young man at the centre of Carlos' story. Using person-first language, this young man might be referred to as a 'pupil with autism,' with the 'autism' being presented in this phrase, as one dimension to his being, rather than central to it. It has been found, however, that 'identify-first' language, which would instead assume the alternative phrase of 'autistic pupil,' is a preference for many within the autistic community (e.g., Kenny et al., 2016). The arguments made for identity-first language are strong. As well as reflecting the views and wishes of many autistic individuals, identity-first language, it has been claimed, does not minimise autism, as person-first language seems to. Just as we tend to use identity-first expressions in relation to queer identities, such as 'lesbian woman' or 'gay man,' terms such as 'autistic person' emphasise how autism is something to be proud of.

Whereas a move from person-first to identity-first language is possibly key to shifting negative attitudes in relation to autism, from my own perspective, it arguably also poses a challenge for the implementation of inclusive practice in education. If we are using identity-first language in school settings, for example, and talking about 'autistic pupils,' are we not simultaneously implying that these pupils form a homogenous group, to be dispensed classroom strategies associated with autism education, that we should expect them all to be responsive to? Do phrases that use identity-first language, such as 'there's two autistic children joining our Reception class next year,' obscure the learning differences between children who share a label, and the multiplicity of different factors impacting upon their participation? Rather than focus educators on questions around what provisionally seems to be 'working' with particular pupils, in a particular moment, and iteratively develop strategies to meet complex individual needs (as Carlos and his colleagues do) does not identity-first language prompt a sense of absolutism, and the passive implementation of what is deemed to generally 'work' for 'autistic learners'? That is not to say, however, that calls to move towards identity-first language, from the autistic community, should be dismissed or rejected. If we are to use identity-first language, however (as I have done, in places, within this chapter), we do need to be mindful that the label 'autistic' is unlikely to capture the full complexity of unique learners and unique learning situations. Whereas identity-first language can be empowering and depict autism positively, it is, therefore, by no means, from a pedagogical perspective, unproblematic.

There are other issues related to the distinction between 'what works' in education and 'what's working?', that are worthy of discussion. If an intervention is found to 'work,' through the findings of an RCT, then we surely also need to also ask 'For whom?' 'For what?' and 'For How Long?'. As Wrigley points out 'aims in education are unsettled, contested and multi-layered. What might impact positively in terms of one aim could be harmful in terms of others' (p. 362). An action may enhance the participation of some pupils and not others. It can enhance independence on one hand, yet undermine learning on the other. As well as a shift away from 'What Works?' in education (and towards the 'Dilemma of What's Working?') this also arguably requires a shift away from utilitarian reasoning, which is based on an assumption that the 'greatest good,' that our actions are anticipated to lead to, is in fact just or 'good' at all.

However, a utilitarian perspective may support Carlos, as a lead practitioner, to think through some of the practicalities around mobilising a team within the school to support James through his anxieties. In order to have five-minute team debriefing sessions about James, at the end of the school day, for example, the two teaching assistants in his class either need to show good will, by working beyond their allocated hours, or have a longer break at times when their presence is needed in the classroom, to deliver the agreed strategies. With this, Carlos needs to consider the needs of other pupils in the school, who themselves require more time with the teaching assistants, yet are also getting increasingly disturbed by James' behaviours, the longer they continue.

In reaching decisions around supporting James and engaging in the 'Dilemma of What's Working?', Carlos and his team were exercising the 'Activist Professionalism,' outlined by Sachs (2000). Sachs writes about how 'joint decision making and new ways of working together' (Sachs, 2000, p. 82) may enable teachers and their associates to challenge the established or 'ritual' practices associated with 'Managerial Professionalism' (2000, p. 86) and bring about a system change that improves 'learning opportunities for all' (p. 93). For Sachs, 'Managerial Professionalism' in education can be a fundamentalist ideology that associates school improvement with the transference of approaches from the private sector. Whereas 'Activist Professionalism' involves continual dialogue and negotiation, 'Managerial Professionalism,' according to Sachs, closes debate down. With 'Managerial Professionalism,' received and established practices are unquestioned, and success is viewed as being contingent upon their effective implementation. Under this definition, 'Managerial Professionalism' therefore arguably has greater coherence with the more abstract question 'What works?' and is detrimental to any authentic interaction with the 'Dilemma of What's Working?'

In outlining her vision for 'Activist Professionalism,' Sachs utilises the concepts of 'active trust' and 'generative politics' from the Sociologist Anthony Giddens. Active trust involves engagement with others, as part of professional practice, and a valuing of the different perspectives that different people bring, which may be different from our own. Generative politics 'allows and encourages individuals and groups to make things happen rather than let things happen to them' (p. 85). Through dialogue and negotiation between various parties (e.g., parents, teachers, young people, or professionals from sectors such as social care), new realities are forged, and the organisation of learning benefits from the multiple insights informing planning, practice development, and decision-making. Central to Sachs' 'Activist Professionalism,' therefore, is an emphasis on the importance of collaboration, such as the collaboration which Carlos and the other members of the team around the young person, 'James,' were undertaking. According to Sachs, 'Managerial Professionalism' is based on individualism.

Carlos' story, about working with James, however, could be interpreted as challenging binary distinctions between Sachs' 'Managerial Professionalism' and 'Activist Professionalism.' Alongside working proactively with colleagues to innovate in ways that challenged a culture of individualism in education, Carlos also found himself adopting a discourse of 'Managerial Professionalism,' reflecting an awareness of his individual professional accountability. As well as in the title which Carlos chose to give his story, 'Managerial Professionalism' can be seen, for example, in terms which he uses, such as 'scrutinised behaviour data.' Rather than a criticism of Carlos' practice, this blending of 'Managerial Professionalism' and 'Activist Professionalism' could be assumed to be a good thing, and a reflection of how, bringing about change and social justice for vulnerable learners such as James, may involve pragmatism, and not necessarily involve a choice between one approach to professional practice, or another.

References

Dettmer, S., Simpson, R. L., Myles, B. S., & Ganz, J. B. (2000). The use of visual supports to facilitate transitions of students with Autism. *Focus on Autism and Other Developmental Disabilities, 15*(3). https://doi.org/10.1177/108835760001500307

Education Endowment Foundation. (2025, 6th May). *EEF Launches update teaching and learning toolkit*. Retrieved November 27, 2021, from https://educationendowmentfoundation.org.uk/about-us

Foran, D., Hoerger, M., Philpott, H., Jones, E. W., Hughes, J. C., & Morgan, J. (2015). Using applied behaviour analysis as standard practice in a UK special needs school. *British Journal of Special Education*, 42(1). https://doi.org/10.1111/1467-8578.12088

Jones, P., & Lawson, H. (2015). Insights into teacher learning about pedagogy from an international group of teachers of students with severe intellectual disabilities. *European Journal of Special Needs Education*, 30(3). https://doi.org/10.1080/08856257.2015.1023000

Kenny, L., Hattersley, C., Molins, B., Buckley, C., Povey, C., & Pellicano, E. (2016). Which terms should be used to describe autism? Perspectives from the UK autism community. *Autism*, 20(4), 442–462. https://doi.org/10.1177/1362361315588200

Kupferstein, H. (2018). Evidence of increased PTSD symptoms in autistics exposed to applied behavior analysis. *Advances in Autism*, 4(1). https://doi.org/10.1108/AIA-08-2017-0016

Pierce, J. M., Spriggs, A. D., Gast, D. L., & Luscre, D. (2013). Effects of visual activity schedules on independent classroom transitions for students with Autism. *International Journal of Disability, Development and Education*, 60(3). https://doi.org/10.1080/1034912X.2013.812191

Sachs, J. (2000). The activist professional. *Journal of Educational Change*, 1, 77–94.

Wrigley, T. (2018). The power of 'evidence': Reliable science or a set of blunt tools? *British Educational Research Journal*, 44(3), 359–376. https://doi.org/10.1002/berj.3338

Chapter 6

Is provision for Annam at our school 'good enough'?

Polly's experience of working with her tutor group at the large comprehensive school where she was employed as a teacher of Religious Education (RE) was an overwhelmingly positive one. It was a complex group that included learners at risk of exclusion, as well as a young person with acute mental health issues, who was accessing intensive support from Child and Adolescent Mental Health Services (CHAMHS). The group also included Annam, who had Severe Learning Difficulties:

> She had severe epilepsy. Her fitting was adding to her brain damage, so every time she had a fit, she sort of regressed further, so her needs were quite extreme. ... She had a one-to-one teaching assistant with her at all times but not always in form time. Annam was **really** high-level need. She was incontinent. She couldn't ever find my classroom.

Throughout the school day, however, whether it was lunchtime, lesson time, or a time for transition between lessons, Polly knew that Annam would be being looked after. She was exceptionally proud of how protective and caring each individual in her tutor group was towards her. It made Polly feel positive about young people and about humanity in general. Learners that you may not expect to, who had associations, outside of school, with gangs and knife crime, treated Annam with the utmost kindness and compassion. For Polly, this was a reminder that young people tend to be innately good, leading her to conclude that 'although kids can be really mean they look after the vulnerable.'

Polly often wondered, however, if the school was doing Annam a 'disservice,' and whether the overall quality of education was 'good enough.' In particular, she wondered whether-or-not the benefits of Annam's presence within her tutor group were one-sided. Whereas she could see that it was beneficial to the other pupils, through the ways in which it positively 'changed the dynamic' within the classroom, she was not sure that it was beneficial for Annam herself.

Polly's concerns about Annam's educational provision are interesting in that they seem to turn any utilitarian arguments against the inclusion of learners in mainstream schools on their head. Whereas it might be claimed that

DOI: 10.4324/9781003540106-9

Annam's placement in a mainstream classroom environment would be detrimental to the majority of pupils, by diverting teacher time away from them, Polly had found that Annam's placement in the mainstream classroom was actually highly beneficial to the majority, whilst possibly not being so for Annam as an individual:

> I think all the other kids in that group definitely benefitted from her being with them because they got to see, help and be mindful of those kinds of differing needs and it brought out all the best bits of them, having Annam in that class. It meant that there wasn't really bullying in the group and there wasn't that sort of unpleasantness because, they just looked out for each other in a different way…but…but…I don't know how much Annam got out of it.

As part of her professional development, Polly spent a day at a local special school, which made her consider whether-or-not Annam would be better placed in this type of setting. At the special school, Polly could see that there were individual pupils working at a much higher level than Annam, who were all seemingly thriving. Would moving Annam to this special school enable her to access more meaningful learning opportunities? Would it provide her with a peer group, within which she would be developing confidence and self-esteem, by being the one who was caring for others?

However, Polly ultimately saw value in Annam being part of her diverse tutor group that was reflective of our diverse society. She could also see that Annam felt a genuine sense of belonging within her mainstream school. She gained a lot, for example, through going on school trips and residentials, and in participating in whole school events such as concerts. These opportunities to interact with other young people, without special educational needs, would most likely not been available to Annam if she were educated at the special school which Polly had visited.

By articulating concerns around whether Annam's education provision, in a mainstream school, was 'good enough,' Polly's story opens up the debate around special schools. In engaging with this debate, for example, we may also ask ourselves if a placement at a mainstream school actually equates to Annam accessing a quality mainstream school experience and education. Although Annam is part of Polly's tutor group, and joins them for some lessons, she also spends a significant proportion of the school week being taught in a small group, with other learners with SLD, with the learning support department. That this happens reflects the findings of Webster (2022), that what appears to be 'inclusion' in mainstream schools can in fact be the opposite. Whereas we may be resistant to placing a young person in a special school, out of concerns about segregating them from the mainstream, simply putting them physically under the roof of a mainstream school building does not mean they will not be segregated.

It could also be argued that placing Annam in a mainstream school means that she is far less likely to access a meaningful curriculum that addresses her priority needs, as a young person with SLD. When being taught in a small group within the learning support department, Annam and her peers tend to go over initial letter sounds in Phonics sessions, and complete basic addition and subtraction problems in sessions focussed on Numeracy. In a special school, however, they would be arguably more likely to be engaging with the 'separate and distinct' approaches for teaching those with SLD, which, according to Imray and Hinchcliffe (2012, p. 150) are essential. They may be more likely to be accessing an alternative curriculum, for learners with SLD, that Imray and Hinchcliffe advocate for. Such a curriculum, it could be argued, offers more purposeful contexts for developing social skills, for example, through the way in which it departs from the national curriculum being taught in mainstream school settings. Rather than engage with subjects such as English or Maths at a very superficial level, Annam and her peers, it could be claimed, may be instead immersing themselves in alternative subjects such as 'The World Around Me' and gaining opportunities for more purposeful and deeper learning.

Annam would often show Polly work that she had completed when working within a classroom within the learning support department, as part of a small group. To support Annam's communication and self-esteem, she was also often given stickers and certificates to take to afternoon registration with Polly, which enabled her to vocalise how well she had done when working within the learning support department, using the limited range of phrases that she had, such as 'I did good.' With this, however, Polly had noted that Annam was presenting fully completed worksheets to her, showing all correct answers. Many of these answers seemed to have been written over the top of pencil, in pen. Also, on the rare occasions when Polly visited Annam in the learning support department, she could also see that the adults there were providing a lot of prompting to the young people and were focussed on the task being completed, rather than on any learning outcomes associated with it. Polly, therefore, doubted that Annam had much of the understanding of number, or of letter sounds, that the completed worksheets were suggesting. For Polly, this added to concerns over whether Annam's education provision was 'good enough.' Would she not be engaging more authentically with learning if placed in that local special school that she had once visited?

The question around whether Annam should be educated within a special or mainstream school could be viewed as a 'dilemma of difference.' On one hand, we want to provide Annam with a bespoke offer of education, such as that possibly offered within a specialist setting, which is responsive to the realities associated with her having SLD. On the other hand, however, we may want to attach stigma to Annam and other young people with SLD by placing them in a special school and representing them as subnormal 'others.'

According to Norwich (2019, p. 2), considerations around the 'dilemma of difference' established the 'basic design of individual identification and assessment system of additional needs' and remains 'the cornerstone of the system' to the present day. In his writings, he traces the dilemma back to the 1978 Warnock Report on 'The Education of Handicapped Children and Young People' (Warnock Committee, 1978), which initially introduced the term 'Special Educational Needs' into the English policy context. The report refers to being 'on the horns of a dilemma' (p. 42), which it responded to by recommending 'inclusion' in mainstream schools as a universal entitlement, unless this was incompatible with access to provision, the education of other children, or the efficient use of resources.

Beyond the 'dilemma of difference,' Polly's struggles over whether Annam's education provision within her tutor group was 'good enough,' alternatively, reflected what could be referred to as the 'Dilemma of Looking' which is one of the dilemmas underpinning the typology of 'Four Dilemmas for Inclusive Practice,' that was elicited from the analysis of 42 'dilemma stories,' shared by teachers with a commitment to inclusive practice, which included this story from Polly.

In narrating her story, Polly did not seem to articulate a 'dilemma of difference.' She was not concerned about a possible stigmatising impact of offering something different or additional to Annam. The members of her tutor group were broadly aware of each other's needs, and diversity was celebrated, rather than hidden. Polly was instead concerned with reaching valid interpretations of what she was finding in apparent evidence of Annam's learning (such as those worksheets) and/or observing in interactions with others. She was asking herself 'Which interpretation of what we are 'seeing' should we be working with; x or y?'. For Polly, it was through 'looking' that we could gauge how helpful or 'good' Annam's offer of education was to her.

When grappling with the 'Dilemma of Looking,' classroom practitioners are often faced with a choice, therefore, between continuing with practices that appear to be effective on the surface (and may be pleasing to various colleagues, senior leaders, parents, and/or inspectors) or refusing to ignore the dissonance between superficial appearance and reality, and change things. On the surface, the sessions within the learning support department did indeed seem to be highly effective. From Polly's perspective, however, these sessions were staged and seemed to only serve the purpose of enabling the adults supporting them to perform their role as learning support educators.

When interacting with the 'Dilemma of Looking?' teachers observe the responses of pupils and/or dynamics within teaching groups, to make sense of what can be 'seen' (or elicited through other senses such as hearing), making efforts to notice what may otherwise be beyond the range of their professional attention. With Annam, this might involve observing the ways in which she plays with counting cubes, for example, and noting her (mis)conceptions around number, which can be revealed from this. It might involve seeing if she recognises any words, which are very familiar to her, such as 'Lunch Time' when printed on laminated cards. Whatever the context or subject, interaction with the 'Dilemma of Looking' also involves practitioner reflection and deliberation. What is observed in the classroom may be highly ambiguous, requiring educators to adopt hypotheses around the point of learning that a young person may be at, and their possible next steps for further development. These hypotheses can then inform the planning of subsequent sessions and be revised through further formative assessments.

Through engaging in the 'Dilemma of Looking' and reaching the conclusion that the activities Annam undertakes within the learning support department within her mainstream secondary school do not offer much value for her, we may reach the conclusion that this young person may be better placed in a specialist education setting. However, arguably, it is the failure of the learning support department to engage with this 'Dilemma of Looking,' rather than her placement within a mainstream secondary school, which means that Annam's educational provision may not be 'good enough.' Even with the 'separate and distinct' approaches advocated for by Imray and Hinchcliffe (2012, p. 150), it could be argued that it is also possible for specialist settings to deliver highly staged sessions, which merely give an appearance that learning is happening. Just as the completed worksheets that Annam presented to Polly, in afternoon registration, most likely reflected the input from adults, photographs of meals that had been cooked, as part of a lesson on food preparation, taught as part of an alternative and specialist life-skills-based curriculum for learners with SLD within a special school, may have been staged and reflect merely the input of adults also. Although Annam may have arguably had a richer experience at her local special school, therefore, a specialist education, designed around needs associated with having SLD, does not, in itself, guarantee this.

For Polly, it is also through adopting a 'fluid' approach to shaping Annam's educational provision that we can work to ensure that it is 'good enough' for her. This may include a reduced timetable, for example, offsite activities, longer lunch and break times, and/or a dual placement at both the specialist and mainstream settings. Rather than adopt a definite position, in relation to the 'special schools' debate' around where young people with SLD should be educated, Polly argues, we should organise bespoke packages of support which do not necessarily commit them to a generic and wholesale placement offer:

> I don't believe in a full timetable necessarily. I do think that if a student has special needs, then there needs to be fluidity in their learning opportunity. For example. they may come in later, they may not do all the subjects, they may choose the things that they like to do best. They may end up doing slightly different activities in the lesson, but within the topic that they're learning, if they're in that lesson. I guess they should get a bit more of a bespoke experience…

However, for Polly, authentic inclusion and following such a 'fluid' approach are undermined by the rigid systems which mainstream secondary schools tend to be required to fit into. Due to the linear nature of the curriculum, for example, missing some lessons whilst going to others may in fact exacerbate difficulties rather than provide support in relation to them. Constraints around staffing and timetabling will inevitably play a greater role in determining where Annam is, at a particular time of day, than the needs outlined within her Education, Health and Care Plan (EHCP). Arguably, specialist settings have a greater capacity to adopt the 'fluid' approach that Polly describes. Having several staff attached to a class, along with staff that work across different classes, for example, offers scope for the creation of different learning groups, for different points in a week, and for targeted activities and interventions. That specialist settings can be more flexible could possibly serve as an argument against mainstream schools for young people with SLD. However, it could also be argued that mainstream schools do not have to be this way and are, in fact, morally obliged to adapt provision around the needs of the young people who enter them.

We must also be cautious before assuming that any concerns about the quality of what is being delivered to Annam, in the learning support department, mean that her placement within the mainstream secondary school has failed. Various writings on inclusive education highlight the elusive, contestable, and ambiguous nature of inclusive classroom practice. It is argued, across the research literature on the principle of Inclusive Pedagogy, for example, that the same action within a classroom can simultaneously strengthen the inclusion of learners, and undermine it (e.g., Florian, 2012, p. 277). Sitting around a table in the learning support department, completing a worksheet, may have, on one hand, been a way of merely keeping Annam busy, to enable the subject teacher, in the mainstream classroom, to focus on the other pupils. More positively, however, it may have also provided a safe space for Annam to practice speech, language, and communication skills, which could then be transferred to her interactions with members of Polly's tutor group, in afternoon registration. Rather than claim that particular classroom practices are 'inclusive', or otherwise, therefore, we arguably need to engage with the 'Dilemma of Looking' and consider the various nuances associated with these practices. This is something which Florian and Black-Hawkins (2011) do in their study into inclusive classrooms in Scottish primary schools, in which they outline, with participating teachers, what is both 'manifest in terms of inclusion' and 'manifest in terms of exclusion' with particular pedagogical approaches (p. 821).

With this in mind, it would be by concluding that Annam's education provision is 'good enough,' that would be doing her a 'disservice.' If we were to decide that everything was entirely fine at school for Annam and did not need to be tweaked or changed, then we are no longer 'looking' at what is happening for her in the classroom. Instead, we are merely implementing abstract practices that might be considered to be inclusive, without 'seeing' the complex and ambiguous ways in which she is responding to them. This resonates with Graham and Slee's (2008) suggestion that the term 'inclusive,' in relation to education, is preferable to the term 'inclusion.' Whereas the term 'inclusion' implies finality and a destination rather than a journey, the term 'inclusive' assumes that the processes of increasing participation in schools are always in continual development. Wherever a young person is educated, it is the absolutism that comes with believing that the job of 'inclusion' has been done (or that comes within the abstract notions of good practice contained within some specialist curricula taught at special schools) that ultimately undermines the quality of education for learners such as Annam, with SLD. Through having doubts, and asking questions, as Polly does, and in engaging in the 'Dilemma of Looking,' the journey of enhancing high-quality education for learners with SLD continues.

References

Department of Education and Science. (1978). *Special Educational Needs: Report of the Committee of Enquiry into the Education of Handicapped Children and Young People (The Warnock Report)*. London, England: Her Majesty's Stationery Office.

Florian, L. (2012). Preparing teachers to work in inclusive classrooms: key lessons for the professional development of teacher educators from scotland's inclusive practice project. *Journal of Teacher Education*, 63(4). https://doi.org/10.1177/0022487112447112

Florian, L., & Black-Hawkins, K. (2011). Exploring inclusive pedagogy. *British Educational Research Journal*, 37(5), 813–828. https://doi.org/10.1080/01411926.2010.501096

Graham, L. J., & Slee, R. (2008). An illusory interiority: Interrogating the discourse/s of inclusion. *Educational Philosophy and Theory*, 40(2). https://doi.org/10.1111/j.1469-5812.2007.00331.x

Imray, P., & Hinchcliffe, V. (2012). Not fit for purpose: A call for separate and distinct pedagogies as part of a national framework for those with severe and profound learning difficulties. *Support for Learning*, 27(4). https://doi.org/10.1111/1467-9604.12002

Norwich, B. (2019). From the warnock report (1978) to an education framework commission: A novel contemporary approach to educational policy making for pupils with special educational needs/disabilities. *Frontiers in Education*, 4. https://doi.org/10.3389/feduc.2019.00072

Webster, R. (2022). *The Inclusion Illusion: How Children with Special Educational Needs Experience Mainstream Schools*. London, England: UCL Press https://doi.org/10.14324/111.9781787357099

Chapter 7

Is it necessary to be creating art in an Art lesson?

Conversations about the quality of teaching and learning are an integral part of Joanne's role as a deputy headteacher within a special school. They underpin dialogues that follow lesson observations, for example, as well as strategic discussions about the direction of curriculum and assessment policy. In such conversations, considerations are raised around what exactly constitutes 'quality' when educating pupils with SPMLD. When evaluating the 'quality' of education, for example, are we essentially looking for very similar things, whatever the profile of the pupils, or the context of the school? Or does teaching pupils with SPMLD require an entire rethink of the notion of 'quality,' as well as a questioning of associated inherited assumptions around what it means for a young person to be schooled?

An attachment to inherited conventions of schooling, which may be rooted in our own childhood experiences, can arguably determine how classrooms with learners with SPMLD are organised and lessons structured. A class of six or seven learners with SPMLD, for example, might all be sitting together in a circle, taking it in turn to tap an interactive whiteboard which flashes in response, in a way that imitates what may be viewed as typically occurring within a mainstream primary or secondary school. For the 20 minutes in which these six or seven learners do not seem to immediately require medical or personal care, the boredom and disconnect of those waiting for their turn to tap the screen, may not be apparent to anyone observing the session, which, on a superficial level, appears to represent a successful effort to establish appropriate conditions for learning. Rather than the needs of the six or seven learners, however, the entire format of the session is shaped by established notions of schooling, which can be arguably traced back to the origins of compulsory education in Victorian Britain. Even in the use of technology in this session, it could be claimed, we have rote learning in a different guise, exemplifying the point that many digital learning tools, for children and young people in schools, often merely reproduces the same old traditional didactic methods, rather than represent an alternative to them (Burns, 2021, p. 29).

In her account of observing a lesson within the special school in which she is a deputy headteacher, Joanna starts to question the assumption that creating artwork is an essential prerequisite of a high-quality Art lesson. Along with other stories from teachers, which featured in the analysis for the research study, it is an account which suggests an association between inclusive classroom practice, and the challenging of received notions of what effective education 'looks like.'

In the Art lesson that Joanne observed, the pupils were not actually engaged in creating artwork. Whereas it could be argued that a necessary component was therefore missing in this lesson, Joanne was impressed by the depths at which pupils were learning. For Joanne, the quality of the lesson came from the holistic observable progress being made by the pupils, rather than from whether-or-not the pupils happened to be doing art activities. Joanne was impressed by how the teacher moved beyond an insistence on art-for-art's-sake and shifted her focus towards the priority learning needs within the classroom. Meeting these needs did not involve creating a beautiful picture, but practicing the required fine motor skills and problem-solving to open pots of paint independently:

> I watched ... I observed last week an Art lesson where there was *no art*. The art didn't happen because that teacher was so skilful and recognised that there was learning that was going on, just from collecting the equipment. It was so valuable. Children were practicing skills such as opening lids. The teacher got these squeezy tubes of paint with a flip lid. One child had got the wrong end and she was trying to open it and the staff stepped back rather than dived in to help her. This allowed the girl to explore it. She explored it and when she finally worked it out she was so thrilled with herself. And so engaged! Another child had to put the lid back on and he only had the use of one arm. ... And he's looking at all the other kids and he's looking around and he can't do it. And then ... you can see a lightbulb moment and he *smacks* the tube down on the table to shut the lid. And I thought 'all that problem-solving! All that thinking for themselves!'
> There may be no piece of art at the end of the lesson but they've just explored those materials and had a really good learning experience!

There are interesting parallels between Joanna's story and a story shared by another educator, 'Annabel,' that was also analysed as part of the research study. This story, titled 'Should Dylan goes to school assemblies?', was centred around various barriers to participation, she encountered in a young boy with SLD and autism, whom she taught in a mainstream primary school, when he was between the ages of three and five. It is a story in which Annabel found herself challenging ways of 'doing things,' in relation to school assemblies, that had evidently not previously been questioned:

> Dylan was always better on a chair, so then everybody sat on a chair. Why were we all sitting cross legged on the floor anyway?

As Dylan's teacher in this story, Annabel became his advocate. In this role, she found herself querying the logic behind embedded systems, processes, and procedures within her school, and pushing for change. In the same way as Joanne, in her story, was initiating a rethink over what constitutes 'quality,' Annabel was initiating a rethink around the 'format of assembly' and how it could be adapted around the needs of Dylan, and also of other children. Rather than hand out paper certificates, for example, children started to be rewarded with colourful ping pong balls to put into transparent tubes. This was both interactive and visually represented, which house within the school that had the most points. Visual prompts and timers were also used. In describing these changes, Annabel emphasises her commitment to adapting around pupils, rather than requiring individual pupils to adapt themselves.

In their stories, therefore, both Joanne and Annabel are change-agents. They are active in redefining inclusive practice and in shaping new realities in relation to it. They are, therefore, also arguably exercising the 'Activist Professionalism' outlined by Sachs (2000) and thinking beyond the culture of 'Managerial Professionalism,' which she contrasts with it, in her writings.

Rather than the 'dilemma of difference,' both Joanna and Annabel, in their stories, are preoccupied with what the research study identified as the 'Dilemma of What Matters?'. Whereas the 'dilemma of difference,' which has long-dominated dialogues around special educational needs (Norwich, 2008, 2019), arises from conflicting desires to provide bespoke support and not stigmatise others by treating them in different ways to everybody else, the 'Dilemma of What Matters?' relates to defining core professional values, establishing moral purpose, and/or evaluating the rationale behind school policies and practices. It is a dilemma, for example, that requires educators to ask questions such as:

- When we talk about 'entitlement' or 'quality' (or any other professional value or concept), do we take it to mean x or y?
- Is a or b more important to the lives of our pupils, and which one should we prioritise through our teaching?

For Joanna and Annabel, in their stories, their 'Dilemma of What Matters?' was around the extent to which received notions of what is appropriate should be challenged and boundaries extended. They were considering whether particular conventions associated with being at school indeed 'mattered' or whether they should be challenged and rejected in the pursuit of enhanced inclusive practices.

So, does producing art in an Art lesson 'matter'? In her reflections, within her story, Joanna makes some important points about the value of the learning process, above the value of any tangible products that teachers and learners may have to show, after the end of a lesson. It may initially look very impressive, for example, for learners to have beautiful Mother's Day or Valentine's cards to take home. However, when these cards look identical to one another, can we actually, with sincerity, refer to them as 'art' in the first place? Does it not instead reflect how the learners have been passively following instructions from adults who have over-prompted them, completed parts of the work on their behalf, and ultimately suppressed their creativity? Does it not reflect a use of time within the school that has had no value whatsoever in relation to the learning and development of children and young people? Could we see these cards as symbolic of a performative school culture, focussed on meeting expectations around what typically happens in school, rather than focussed on challenging these expectations and asking 'What matters?'.

There is an argument that opportunities for artistic expression do indeed 'matter' and that it would be problematic for teaching and learning to start and end with a focus on practical tasks, such as opening tubes of paint, without there being a broader purpose, context, or goal. One of the 'Ten Central Capabilities' which Nussbaum (2011) proposes in her writings, when responding to the question 'What is each person able to be?', is 'Senses, Imagination and Thought' (p. 33). This capability includes cultural experiences and opportunities for creative expression. Nussbaum's set of 'Ten Central Capabilities' offers a framework to support development planning, around the goal of maximising what Nussbaum refers to as 'human flourishing' (Nussbaum, 2009, p. 345). Nussbaum's writings have been applied to considerations relating to the education of those with intellectual disabilities, with Rogers (2013), for example, arguing that 'socially just' (2013, p. 988) practices arise from professional interaction with ethical frameworks such as the Capabilities Approach, rather than from an over-preoccupation with any technical aspects of pedagogy. With reference to Nussbaum, therefore, and with the notion that 'Senses, Thought and Imagination' is a central capability, or fundamental human freedom, we might assert that eventual opportunities to create artwork (for example in the subsequent Art lesson) are important to the young people that Joanna observed. Without such opportunities, would not the challenge of opening and closing a tube of paint be dull, monotonous, and ultimately lacking in significance and meaning?

Globally, and historically, the approach of 'task analysis' has long underpinned the education of very young children in early years settings and/or learners with special educational needs (e.g., Gold, 1976; Schworm, 1979; Tan, Hughes and Toogood, 2016). In the context of special education, the approach of task analysis typically involves breaking down a life skill, such as using a knife and fork (or opening a lid to a tube of paint) into its constituent parts, including all the conceptual understanding and knowledge (that tends to be assumed to mostly be explicitly teachable) to complete it. An example of this approach can be seen in the below text, taken from a PowerPoint slide I once encountered in a training session about school 'OFSTED' inspections, which broke down the 'task' of learning to use a 'potty' or toilet:

- *Are they able to control their bladder or bowels? (tick)*
- *Do they recognise when they want to use the potty? (tick)*

- *Can they communicate when they want to use the potty? (tick)*
- *Can they sit on the potty? (tick)*
- *Can they stay in place long enough to finish using the potty? (tick)*

Whereas learning to use a toilet or potty is an obvious enabler in relation to another of the Ten Central Capabilities on Nussbaum's list, of 'Bodily Integrity,' and whereas task analysis has a likely valuable role to play in maximising the functioning of individuals with SPMLD, it is arguably also important to remember that learning the component parts of a task, in isolation from the bigger picture of the overall task itself, can be problematic. A child can be taught words for communicating that they would like to go on the potty one day, only to have forgotten them on the day that they are being taught how to sit on the potty. A young person may struggle to transfer abstract guidance on how to open a tube of paint to actually painting. In my experience, rather than being explicitly taught, knowledge and skills to complete tasks are usually acquired in context and involve the individual finding their own unique short-cuts and ways of doing things, rather than conforming to a set of pre-defined steps that have been established by others. In the Art lesson that Joanna observed, the learner who found himself slamming the tube of paint down, in order to use it, apparently did have a context and, rather than being taught to follow such pre-defined steps, was finding a way that works around him, only having the use of one arm. However, to embrace the full humanity of each young person and child within the classroom, in relation to each and every one of Nussbaum's Ten Central Capabilities, education arguably needs to strive to do more than merely teach functional life skills, and measure progress in relation to the successful completion of each step towards doing them. It also arguably needs to view the learning of functional life skills holistically, in ways that relate to all aspects of an individual's being, that cannot simply be broken down into a list.

In the same way as the format of school assemblies, which Annabel first encountered when teaching Dylan, replicated and reproduced conventions associated with traditional schooling, the approach of task analysis, with very young children and learners with special educational needs, arguably does exactly the same. Parallels can be drawn, for example, between the way in which 'task analysis' focusses on the explicit teaching of 'steps' towards a task, and the emphasis, within the 2014 National Curriculum for England and Wales, on subject-specific content knowledge, which is broken down into age expectations for each year group or phase of education. The approach of task analysis, for teaching very young children, or those with SEN, also has coherence with the emphasis on direct instruction within dominant discourses related to the teaching of this content knowledge. With both task analysis and the notion of teaching subject content through direct instruction, the teacher is arguably conceptualised as the imparter of specific knowledge. With this in mind, what we are seeing in the PowerPoint slide on potty training, therefore, is an attempt to mould teaching and learning, which is holistic and/or developmental in nature, in ways that emulate the traditional and/or mainstream paradigm. Although learning to use a potty or toilet is clearly something that 'matters' to the overwhelming majority of children and young people (some may, for example, have had a stoma fitted) the way in which it is broken down into 'teach-able' steps is more consistent with the role of the 'Managerial Professional' outlined by Sachs, rather than the 'Activist Professional.' It reproduces conventional practices rather than strives towards the 'socially just' practices, which Rogers (2013, p. 988) associates with ethical frameworks such as the Capabilities Approach.

Perhaps, therefore, the question should not be around whether-or-not learners should be creating art within an Art lesson, but around whether-or-not the overall offer of education they have access to serves to maximise their capacity for full 'human flourishing' (Nussbaum, 2009, p. 345).

References

Burns, M. (2021). *Background Paper Prepared for the Global Education Monitoring Report, Technology and Education: Technology in Education.* Paris: UNESCO. Retrieved from https://unesdoc.unesco.org/ark:/48223/pf0000378951

Gold, M. W. (1976). Task analysis of a complex assembly task by the retarded blind. *Exceptional Children, 43*(2). https://doi.org/10.1177/001440297604300203

Norwich, B. (2008). Dilemmas of difference, inclusion and disability: International perspectives on placement. *European Journal of Special Needs Education, 23*(4). https://doi.org/10.1080/08856250802387166

Norwich, B. (2019). From the warnock report (1978) to an education framework commission: A novel contemporary approach to educational policy making for pupils with special educational needs/disabilities. *Frontiers in Education, 4.* https://doi.org/10.3389/feduc.2019.00072

Nussbaum, M. (2011). *Creating Capabilities: The Human Development Approach.* Cambridge, Massachusetts: The Belknap Press of Harvard University Press.

Nussbaum, M. (2009). The capabilities of people with cognitive disabilities. In *Metaphilosophy, 40* (3–4). https://doi.org/10.1111/j.1467-9973.2009.01606.x

Rogers, C. (2013). Inclusive education and intellectual disability: A sociological engagement with Martha Nussbaum. *International Journal of Inclusive Education, 17*(9), 988–1002. https://doi.org/10.1080/13603116.2012.727476

Sachs, J. (2000). The activist professional. *Journal of Educational Change, 1,* 77–94.

Schworm, R. (1979). Task analysis in special education: Definition and clarification. *Journal of Special Education Technology, 2*(3). https://doi.org/10.1177/016264347900200305

Tan, H. C., Hughes, M. R., & Toogood, S. (2016). Using task analysis to promote engagement in special educational settings. *European Journal of Behavior Analysis, 17*(2). https://doi.org/10.1080/15021149.2016.1247575

Chapter 8

Should pupils with PMLD be taught in age-based or needs-based provision?

The very large special school where Joanne is a deputy head teacher has a proportion of pupils with Profound and Multiple Learning Difficulties (PMLD). The needs of these pupils are varied and complex. Their communication is mostly pre-intentional, and the developmental milestones that they are working on tend to be those typically associated with early infancy, such as responding to their own name. Many pupils with PMLD at the school have sensory impairments, life-limiting conditions, and/or complex physical disabilities. When in school, they require intimate personal care. They are also likely to require the administration of medicines and/or medical procedures, manual handling, and/or support with self-harming behaviours.

At Joanne's school, pupils move through each of the age phases, starting off in 'Lower School' and then moving into the 'Middle' and 'Upper' Schools. Joanne is unsure over whether this is helpful for pupils with PMLD, with each transition moving them away from those familiar adults, who have reached highly nuanced insights into their needs over time. Although it may appear to be more inclusive to have pupils with PMLD moving up through the school alongside pupils without PMLD, Joanne questions whether-or-not it is the best thing to do:

> If those children with PMLD rely so much on their staff team understanding their subtle communications, and knowing those children in depth, then is it right to take them away from that team to move up into the next school? The philosophy behind our curriculum for PMLD learners is that the child is the curriculum! That's the philosophy of our curriculum, so relationships are key. We start with the children, the child's needs, and then their personalised learning grows from that. It takes a long time to get to know all those little subtle signs, things like which side a learner needs to be on to be more comfortable, or how far away she needs to be able to see something … all those things. …
>
> So, is moving the children up to be with their age-related peers the right thing to do? Or should I keep them with the same team with the same teacher in the same room and then have mixed age-group classes, so as children leave, new children fill those spaces

DOI: 10.4324/9781003540106-11

In asserting that 'the child is the curriculum,' Joanne is arguing that each individual with PMLD has a bespoke offer of education, that is unique to particular priorities for their learning and development. For very many young people with PMLD, for example, it might be a priority to build anticipation in relation to familiar stimuli, in order to maximise overall engagement. For some, learning activities that provide opportunities to learn to crawl or bottom-shuffle would be beneficial. In the argument that the 'child is the curriculum,' therefore, the idea is that the content of what the child is taught comes from them, rather than from documents outlining a body of knowledge that they must work through. It is an argument largely associated with the pioneering work of Chailey Heritage School in Sussex, who place the phrase 'the child is the curriculum' at the centre of their curriculum policy (Chailey Heritage School, 2018).

As is the case in Joanne's reflection, above, the claim that 'the child is the curriculum' can potentially prompt a rethink over whether-or-not placing young people with PMLD in classes with other young people who are their own age is necessary. Due to the complexity of their needs, classes with only learners with PMLD can be very small, and typically, in my experience, have around eight students or fewer, with at least three staff members. If each individual child within such classes is following a personalised curriculum, shaped by them, then there is an argument that the age of the other learners, who are physically in the room with them, is irrelevant. If whole class teaching isn't happening, and the different learners in the class are not doing the same thing anyway, does moving learners with PMLD up through the school as they get older actually matter?

However, if the child, within a special school, really *is* the curriculum, do we not in fact have an argument for doing the opposite to what Joanne, in her story, is considering as an option? Rather than keep learners with PMLD within the same mixed-aged class throughout their entire time in school, would it not be more appropriate to create more generic age-based classes in which they learn alongside those without PMLD (possibly including those with more moderate learning difficulties)? If very different individuals, at very different points of learning, are simultaneously following an individualised curriculum, rather than all being taught the exact same thing as a whole class, then is not the bringing together of those with PMLD, and those with much higher levels of prior attainment, more feasible? Although it is exceptionally rare for a school to create such diverse groups (and I have actually only ever encountered one that has), does this not have its benefits, and might these benefits outweigh the perceived benefits to those with PMLD of having the same staff working with them throughout their entire time in school? In a research study, Simmons (2021) found that, for children with PMLD, opportunities to interact with peers of the same age, without PMLD, during visits to a mainstream school, supported significant learning and development, which surpassed the expectations of adults. Would not doing the opposite of what

Joanne is considering, and organising learners into diverse age-based groups, rather than groups based on needs, potentially do the same?

Practically speaking, however, there is, in reality, an extent to which schools have very little flexibility around how to organise their classes. Bringing diverse learners together may be an appropriate thing to do in some specialist settings, and reap exponential benefits, yet in others it may compromise safeguarding and pose a considerable risk to the most vulnerable. The options that school leaders then have when creating class groups, will be inevitably limited. It would be difficult, for example, to place a pre-verbal adolescent who regularly throws objects and knocks items over, alongside a learner who relies on respiratory equipment that needs to be kept in place throughout the entire day. In small school settings in particular, school leaders may even find that they are left with no choices to make around how to constitute class groups. Once all the immediate risks are mitigated, they might find that they are left with a precarious and pragmatic arrangement that they can see no real alternative to. Such an arrangement may mean that the classes do indeed span across different age groups. Usually, however, in my own experience, classes tend to be created that include learners at ages that are all within two or three years of one another, making the suggestion from Joanna, of having classes that might include children between the ages of 2 and 19, a fairly radical one.

Rather than plan in relation to the principle that the child themselves is the curriculum, schools have the option of adopting curricula that have been specifically designed around the labels 'Moderate Learning Difficulties' (MLD), 'Severe Learning Difficulties' (SLD), and 'Profound and Multiple Learning Difficulties' (PMLD). Whereas the national curriculum for England is age-based, outlining content for children and young people to learn in each phase of their education, such curricula are needs-based. Alternative needs-based curricula have been developed within schools (e.g., Swiss Cottage, 2025) and are also available for education settings to purchase as commercial products (EQUALS, 2025). If schools take the option of working with needs-based curricula (e.g., by implementing a 'Sensory Curriculum' for learners with PMLD and/or a 'Semi-Formal Curriculum' for learners with SLD, which focusses on the teaching of life-skills), then, in turn, priorities for how teaching groups are constituted are established. If all learners with SLD, for example, are following a 'Semi-Formal Curriculum,' which is made up of subjects such as 'The World About Me,' that have been designed around needs associated with having SLD, then it logically makes sense to create specific SLD classes, that are equipped with appropriate resources, and staffed by educators deemed to have related expertise. If all learners with PMLD are following a related needs-based curriculum, made up of subjects such as 'Sensory Engagement,' it then also makes sense to create classes that are specifically for learners with PMLD. An emphasis on needs-based curricula, therefore, is likely to raise questions similar to those which Joanna grapples with, and represent a challenge to any assumptions that learners should necessarily be grouped according to their age. Such questions arguably position Joanna, along with those advocating for alternative needs-based curricula (e.g., Imray and Hinchcliffe, 2013) as 'Activist Professionals' (Sachs, 2000), who initiate a rethink of established practices, that have a basis in tradition, rather than a basis in considerations around what is in the best interests of children and young people.

There is an extent to which, however, the creation of needs-based classes in schools, to enable the teaching of needs-based curricula, can also be problematic. Hypothetically, a 15-year-old, for example, might have complex physical disabilities and a life-limiting condition, alongside the label 'SLD,' and a capacity to 'sight-read' high-frequency words on posters around her school, which surpasses the level that many learners with the label 'MLD' are currently working at. The most appropriate class for this learner, however, seems to be with learners with PMLD, and one other learner who has the label of SLD, who is also medically fragile. The school does have a class for learners with prior attainment that seems to fall between the levels associated with having SLD and PMLD, but the adolescents in this class are very physical in their behaviours, making it difficult to establish the conditions that this 15-year-old requires in order to be safe on a daily basis. Also, hypothetically, in the same education setting, a ten-year-old with cerebral palsy, autism, and the label 'SLD' (that has been queried by teaching staff due to them having a relatively good understanding of numbers) may be in a class with other learners with SLD, and following a life-skills-based curriculum, in Year 6. For the following year, however, Year 7, additional learners have joined the school, meaning that numbers within that same class, moving up, are beyond capacity. Senior Leaders are also keen to respond to concerns around having particular combinations of learners together, raised by staff and parents. This ten-year-old, therefore (about to turn eleven), moves out of the teaching group designated for learners with 'Severe Learning Difficulties,' following a 'Semi-Formal Curriculum' and into a class designated for learners with 'Moderate Learning Difficulties,' following an adapted national curriculum.

Rather than the child being the curriculum, therefore, it can be pragmatic factors, which ultimately determine the educational experience which young people receive. Although a school may reach a decision over whether to adopt an age-based or needs-based approach, the reality of what children are accessing may ultimately end up being neither one nor the other.

Needs-based approaches to teaching those with SPMLD tend to be based on the principle of 'stage-not-age.' Needs-based curricula for learners with SPMLD, therefore, do not necessarily outline what is taught at particular age groups. Instead, such needs-based curricula are often based on a recognition that an individual can be working on a developmental milestone, which may typically be reached in early infancy, at any age. Broadly speaking, however, the balance between learner age and learner need (in shaping a curriculum deemed appropriate to individual children and young people with special educational needs) tends to shift, according to perceptions around their ability. The more academically proficient a learner with SEN is seen to be, the more their curriculum is viewed as being required to reflect how old they are. A curriculum designed for 'Moderate Learning Difficulties,' therefore, is more likely to have different subjects and content for different age groups. This is less likely to be the case with a curriculum designed exclusively for learners with PMLD. With this in mind, we may start to question, as Joanna does, whether-or-not there is any value in moving learners with PMLD up through the school, as they get older.

The dilemma that Joanna outlines, between moving young people with PMLD up through the school, and the alternative of keeping them within the mixed-age, needs-based class in which they seem settled, could be viewed as a 'dilemma of difference.' The 'dilemma of difference' has been featured extensively across academic and policy dialogues related to special educational needs and disabilities (e.g., Norwich, 2008, 2010) and is concerned with having a desire to meet individual needs in individualised ways, whilst also wanting to avoid stigmatising individuals by treating them differently from others. If conceptualising Joanna's dilemma as a 'dilemma of difference,' then moving learners with PMLD between 'Lower,' 'Middle,' and 'Upper' school might be assumed to have value through the way in which it represents a normative experience of education. Having mixed-age PMLD classes might also be assumed to have value, through the capacity it brings to strengthening personalised provision. In reality, however, it is not necessarily the case that both of these assumptions are correct, in which case we arguably do not in fact have a 'dilemma of difference' at all.

Rather than a 'dilemma of difference,' the predicament which Joanna describes, between moving learners with PMLD up the school, and keeping them within the same mixed-aged class could be viewed as a 'Dilemma of What Matters?'. This is a dilemma found across a number of the 42 'dilemma stories' from teachers, which were analysed alongside Joanna's story. It is a dilemma related to evaluating the rationale behind school policies and practices, establishing moral purpose, and/or defining core professional values. For Joanna, in this story, 'relationships are key' to the lives of individuals with PMLD, meaning that maintaining secure bonds with practitioners arguably 'matters' more than being with age equivalent peers within the same teaching group.

Joanna's story is also situated within wider discussions about the professional value of 'age appropriateness' (Forster, 2010) and the extent to which it 'matters' when planning for individuals with PMLD. Forster (2010) links discourses on age appropriateness to conventional social roles and a desire to 'normalise' individuals with PMLD in relation to them. For Joanna, moving pupils with PMLD from Lower School to Middle School was possibly seen by Joanna to be valuing 'age appropriateness' above the benefits of giving them ongoing access to adults who can confidently respond to, and advocate for their needs, because they know them. This makes her story a very interesting one in which engagement with the 'Dilemma of What Matters?' involves simultaneously challenging conventional notions of school and addressing Aristotelian or 'Nussbaumian' questions around the 'good life' and appropriate conditions for 'human flourishing' (Nussbaum, 2009, p. 345). In the same way as another story analysed for the study, 'Is Katie Being Under the Table an Issue?' challenges the assumption that school involves pupils sitting at a desk, this story from Joanna asks whether organising learning around chronological ages is necessarily beneficial for everyone. For Joanna, rather than emulate received notions of what a school 'is,' strategic education planning should begin with the actual needs of actual pupils.

In Joanna's story, it is practitioners 'knowing' their pupils that is deemed to 'matter.' Whilst this feels impossible to disagree with, however, we must remember that there is a difference between 'knowing' and 'looking.' Within this typology of dilemmas, established through the analysis of the stories, the *Dilemma of 'Looking'* was also identified. This dilemma involves practitioners grappling with their professional perceptions, values, and attitudes, as well as their conceptions of where truth is located within a classroom. When engaging in this 'Dilemma of Looking?' therefore, educators may be considering questions such as:

- What are these behaviours suggesting to us?
- Which interpretation of what we are 'seeing' should we be working with, x or y?

Arguably, if we claim to 'know' pupils (or decide a priori that something 'matters'), this continual hermeneutic process of assessment and planning stops, and we no longer 'see' any responses from pupils that challenge any assumptions that we have formed about them. It is valuing the Dilemma of 'Looking' that arguably makes the 'Dilemma of What Matters?' an actual 'dilemma' rather than the defence of an absolutist opinion on what should happen within a school. In relation to Joanna's situation and reaching decisions on how to arrange learners with PMLD into groups, there is also an argument that effective and sustainable provision, in the long term, requires something more than adults, who have worked with individuals for years, 'knowing' them. Whereas knowledge around individual needs, accumulated over time, is a fantastic resource in a classroom with learners with PMLD, we surely have to aim to disseminate strategies for supporting learning, so that success does not rely on only a small handful of staff who have this knowledge. Another priority for Joanna and her team would be preparing the young people for working with a range of educators and carers across their life course, and for being in different environments. Moving learners with PMLD up through the school would support this priority and would also arguably support the conditions through which educators are going beyond asserting that they 'know' their pupils, and engaging in the 'Dilemma of Looking?'. What does it mean to 'know' a pupil anyway, and should we not instead embrace what we don't know, and situate ourselves as learners ourselves, in relation to them?

Ultimately, however, if we are to engage with both the 'Dilemma of What Matter's?' and the 'Dilemma of Looking?', we may conclude, as Joanna does, that we may not, after all, have to make a binary choice between age-based and needs-based teaching groups. Instead, schools can opt for a more fluid and flexible arrangement, in which there is scope for learners to dip in and out of different activities, led by different adults, in different classrooms, within a cross-phase PMLD department:

> My vision is that we have the PMLD children in the centre of the school next to the hydro pool with their own therapy room, so that there can actually be free-flow between those three classes. So, one group might be working on physical development. They might be having a 'Move' session. With another group, there might be a sensory story going on, so it's all one big department

This vision, which Joanne articulates, may be logistically difficult, and questions may remain around learners with needs that fall between that offered by such a cross-phase PMLD department, and needs that might be addressed by a life skills-based curriculum, designed for learners with SLD, taught within an entirely different part of the school. Significantly, however, it is a vision for an arrangement that is likely to avoid any passivity which may come with staff remaining attached to the same PMLD pupils, whom they claim to 'know,' and repeating the same routine practices, rather than continually enhancing them. It is an arrangement that offers scope for teaching and learning to be dynamic and establish the 'new ways of working' which Sach's (2000, p. 82) associates with what she terms 'Activist Professionalism.'

References

Chailey Heritage School. (2018). *Chailey Heritage Individual Learner Driven Curriculum: "The CHILD is the curriculum"*. Retrieved from https://www.chf.org.uk/The_CHILD_Curriculum_-_March_2018.pdf Accessed on: May102025

EQUALS. (2025, 6th May). *Curriculum Schemes of Work from EQUALS*. http://equals.co.uk/curriculum/

Forster, S. (2010). Age-appropriateness: Enabler or barrier to a good life for people with profound intellectual and multiple disabilities? *Journal of Intellectual and Developmental Disability*, 35(2). https://doi.org/10.3109/13668251003694606

Imray, P., & Hinchcliffe, V. (2013). *Curricula for Teaching Children and Young People with Severe or Profound and Multiple Learning Difficulties: Practical Strategies for Educational Professionals*. London, England: Routledge. https://doi.org/10.4324/9781315883298

Norwich, B. (2008). Dilemmas of difference, inclusion and disability: International perspectives on placement. *European Journal of Special Needs Education*, 23(4). https://doi.org/10.1080/08856250802387166

Norwich, B. (2010). Dilemmas of difference, curriculum and disability: International perspectives. *Comparative Education*, *46*(2). https://doi.org/10.1080/03050061003775330

Nussbaum, M. (2009). The capabilities of people with cognitive disabilities. In *Metaphilosophy*, *40*(3–4). https://doi.org/10.1111/j.1467-9973.2009.01606.x

Sachs, J. (2000). The activist professional. *Journal of Educational Change*, *1*, 77–94.

Simmons, B. (2021). The production of social spaces for children with profound and multiple learning difficulties: a Lefebvrian analysis. *British Journal of Sociology of Education*, *42*(5–6). https://doi.org/10.1080/01425692.2021.1922269

Swiss Cottage School, D. and R. C. (2025, 10th May). *Curriculum*. Retrieved from https://swisscottage.camden.sch.uk/learning/curriculum

Part 3

Developing ethical and inclusive teachers

Chapter 9

Towards a topographical pedagogy

The research study, which largely forms the basis of this book, eventually arrived at the metaphor of 'topography' for teaching learners with SPMLD. Above any specialist knowledge, for teaching 'special' learners, the study found a 'topographical' mindset in the various 'dilemma stories' which it analysed, which were shared by and/or crafted with participating teachers. This mindset is analogous to that adopted by cartographers or landscape artists. It involves the observation and exploration of terrain (which in the case of teachers would be the classroom and the communities around the classroom) and developing practice in ways that authentically represent it.

Through arriving at the metaphor of 'topography,' for inclusive practice with those with SPMLD, the notion of 'Topographical Teaching' was developed, as a concept to guide the implementation of inclusive pedagogies. This chapter will outline this notion of 'Topographical Teaching' and discuss its implications for developing SPMLD-inclusive education provision. It will also discuss some additional features of inclusive practice for learners with SPMLD, that were also elicited through an analysis of the teachers' 'dilemma stories.'

As discussed in earlier chapters within this book, an analysis of 42 stories from experienced teachers led to the development of a typology of 'Four Dilemmas for Inclusive Practice.' This typology is outlined in Figure 9.1. The dilemmas within this typology go beyond the 'dilemma of difference' which has been written about extensively in the literature on special educational needs, and inclusive education, and involves a perceived tension between a commitment to addressing the needs of individuals with SEND and a commitment to not stigmatising these pupils by singling them out as being different (Norwich 2008, 2010).

In addition to being analysed to elicit a typology of Four Dilemmas for Inclusive Practice,' that are outlined in Figure 9.1, the below research question was also addressed through the research study:

> What is inclusive pedagogical practice with learners with Severe and/or profound and Multiple Learning Difficulties and/or learners at risk of exclusion?

DOI: 10.4324/9781003540106-13

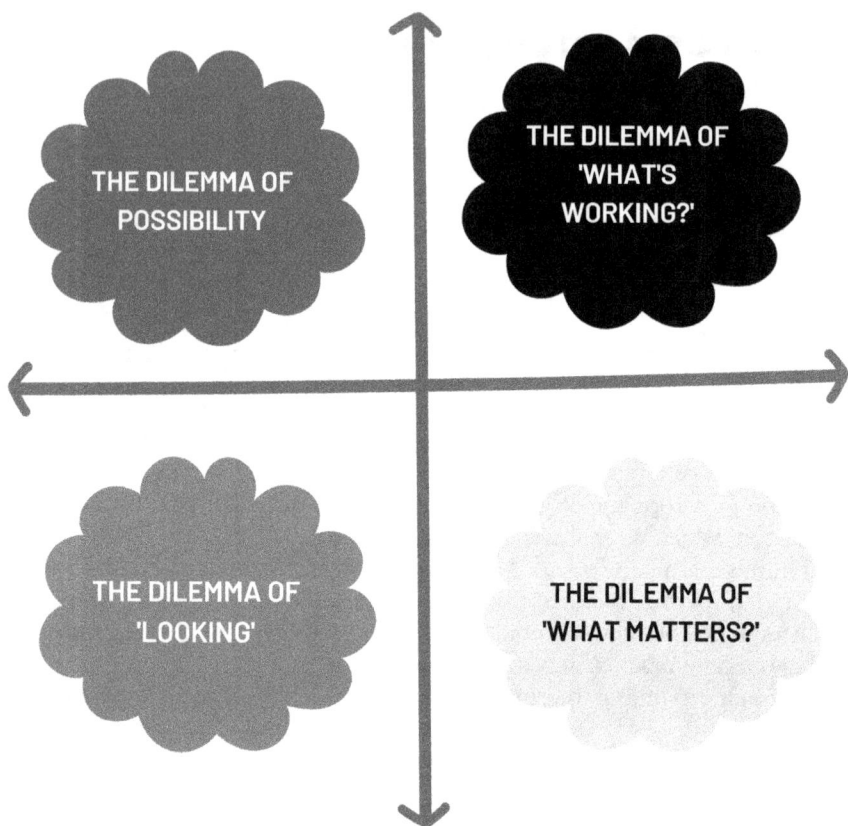

Figure 9.1 A Typology of 'Four Dilemmas for Inclusive Practice.'

A total of 24 of the 42 'dilemma stories,' which featured in the analysis, involved learners with SPMLD, and 38 of the 42 stories were analysed in relation to this research question.

When addressing this research question, the stories were analysed, utilising the approaches proposed by van Manen (2016) in his 'Phenomenology of Practice.' Phenomenological research is concerned with articulating lived experience(s) of the phenomenon under investigation. In relation to this particular study, the phenomenon under investigation was 'inclusive practice with learners at risk of exclusion and/or with SPMLD.' From a phenomenological perspective, therefore, the study was interested in realities associated with being a teacher of these learners, who was committed to delivering 'inclusion,' as defined by Booth and Ainscow, 2002, p. 3) as maximising 'learning and participation.' In phenomenology, these realities tend to be referred to as 'essences' (Merleau-Ponty, 2013, p. 31). Modern phenomenological research, therefore, often involves a quest to reveal the 'essence(s)' of whatever phenomenon is being explored as part of a research study.

Van Manen's approaches to phenomenology are underpinned by processes for interpretation and reflection. Using these approaches, the 'dilemma stories,' analysed for this research study, were discussed at conferences to enable interaction with diverse perspectives on them. All discussions were logged and the research therefore involved having a 'conversation with the situation' (Schon, 1991, pp. 76–104) within each story.

A phenomenological analysis of the stories from teachers, relating to learners with SPMLD, found that the lived experience of inclusive practice with these learners tends to involve the following:

1. Feeling a sense of professional agency
2. Having positive wellbeing
3. Feeling connected to, and collaborating with others
4. Seeing through a 'topographical' lens

This chapter will go through each of these four features (or 'essences') in turn, exemplifying each one with details from specific stories.

Feeling a Sense of Professional Agency

Across the stories, effective and inclusive pedagogical practice with learners with complex needs tended to be associated with teachers having the agency to make reasoned professional judgements and enact pedagogical decisions with a degree of autonomy. This can be seen, for example, in the story 'How can I support Jane to feel positive about teaching learners with Profound and Multiple Learning Difficulties' in which 'Helen,' a deputy head teacher within a diverse special school, sees an exponential increase in the levels of motivation of one of the teachers in her team, 'Jane.' Helen attributes this to the way in which a move towards working with the 'Engagement Model' represented an invitation to Jane to exercise her professional agency.

Using the Engagement Model (Standards and Testing Agency, 2024), teachers observe, assess, and evaluate pupil learning in relation to five 'Areas of Engagement': Exploration, Realisation, Anticipation, Persistence, and Initiation. For Jane, in Helen's story, this required her to authentically exercise her professionalism in ways that enthused her. For Helen, therefore, teacher agency is the golden nugget for strengthening inclusive practice. At times, she claims, 'external pressures that are really toxic' and can undermine this agency, requiring school leaders and policy developments (such as the introduction of the Engagement Model), which restore it:

> She sees what she is doing now as meaningful and purposeful. She understands it in the round, if you like. She can see that everything happening in her classroom is for the children … that we want them to get better at things … So, there's a coherent narrative for her. She fully believes in what she is doing.

Before encountering the 'Engagement Model,' Jane had been acting out of a perceived compliance with external expectations and saw herself as a mere implementer of prescribed approaches. Through using the 'Engagement Model,' however, Jane's sense of professional identity changed, and she found herself actively using her 'practical wisdom' (Florian and Beaton 2018, p. 873) to engage in problem-solving around the real needs of her learners:

> I think that with the engagement model she (Jane) was given enough space. I've always been interested in space. I wrote an article once on the space around the child … but I think here it was about creating space – or I suppose I mean thinking time – around the teacher …

In another story that featured in the analysis 'What have I learnt from teaching that challenging class?' Joanne, a deputy head teacher from another special school, reflects on how she gained the confidence to apply her professional judgement, which first enabled her to make appropriate pedagogical decisions to maximise the learning and participation of her most vulnerable pupils. Her story gives an account of teaching a group earlier in her career, in which all learners had both a diagnosis of autism and the label SLD. Most of the learners were also pre-verbal. Some 'would climb or jump on furniture' or 'pull the trees up' in the playground. For Joanne, practice with this group tended to be ineffective when it was modelled on what she felt she 'should' be doing. It was only by having the agency to shape learning around her professional judgement that the pupils in the group could flourish:

> Now that I'm in a leadership position, I have the courage to do things my own way. Back then, I would have that fear of lesson observation, so would try and make sure that all the children were sat down. I would think 'I should be delivering an introduction; I should have clear learning objectives and those children should be making demonstrable progress during the lesson'. However, that wasn't going to work for those children! It wasn't what they were about. I remember one observation. It was my first observation with the new head. He walked in and one of the kids punched him, somebody else took all their clothes off and that was it! Lesson over! It was because I was trying to do what I felt was expected of me as a classroom practitioner.

Both Joanne's and Helen's stories highlight the negative consequences of teachers being denied professional agency, as well as the stark contrast between being granted this agency and not being granted it. From my own personal perspective, both stories also serve as a reminder to schools to focus efforts on maximising teacher agency, rather than on insisting on the implementation of one approach to the education of SPMLD learners over another. In Helen's story, the use of the Engagement Model is a highly positive thing, which energises a previously demotivated classroom practitioner. However, as much as the Engagement Model, and the ethos behind it, can serve as an invitation to classroom teachers to exercise their professional agency, we need to be cautious before assuming that it will necessarily always perform this role. It is possible that, under a performative school culture, using the model becomes merely a bureaucratic task. Rather than a tool through which teachers apply their professional agency to evaluate the progress that has been made, it becomes a tool for merely 'demonstrating' or 'showing' pupil progress, and disempowers teachers as a result. This is something which has arguably already happened in the use of the Engagement Model in some schools, and which can be seen in some of the toolkits related to it, I have encountered, that are available for schools to purchase. Although certain curriculum and assessment frameworks and/or pedagogical approaches, therefore, offer scope to restore teacher agency, it is important to be mindful of how these same approaches are capable of doing the very opposite. With this in mind, school leaders in settings where there are learners with SPMLD must, it could be argued, avoid any insistence that teachers merely emulate what is deemed to be effective in other schools and fully engage them in more contextualised decision-making.

Having Positive Wellbeing

An analysis of the stories suggests a relationship between inclusive practice with learners with complex needs and the self-confidence and wellbeing of teachers. Self-confidence, for example, enabled Helen and her colleague to be relaxed about non-conformity in the classroom in the story 'Is Katie being under the table an issue?' rather than perceive it as a threat, that needed to be overcome, to establish some authority. In another story, 'Is provision for Annam in my tutor group good enough?', a link between inclusive classroom practice and having a positive outlook is evident. In this story, 'Polly,' a Religious Education teacher in a secondary school within a local authority where young people with SLD typically attend mainstream provision, finds that she needs to hold a balanced view of her form group, rather than interpret their behaviours with suspicion. When going into school each day, Polly does not start with the assumption that young people will inevitably be malicious towards a young person with SLD and instead assumes that those in her form are inherently altruistic. To strengthen inclusion, therefore, Polly adopts a positive outlook on life itself, viewing the young people around her as supportive, rather than as hinderances to be 'managed':

> My old form group were very spirited. They were sweet and generous and their needs hugely differed because quite a few of them were beginners in English. There was one girl in the class for example, who had recently come from Poland who didn't have much English at all. We had another student

who, at the very end of the year, was diagnosed with Asperger's and had some severe mental health issues that were linked to sexuality. Her life was properly in danger, it was a really difficult time ... There was a lot of vulnerable kids in one group which I think can happen sometimes ... Although kids can be really mean, they know when there's a line and I think that they look after the vulnerable. They notice if someone needs taking care of and they make sure they are taken care of ... whatever kid. It may be one that's on the verge of exclusion. It doesn't matter ... They take care of them.

With self-confidence and a requisite level of wellbeing, the teachers in the stories value their encounters with learners who have challenged them, rather than look back on these encounters as negative experiences. This is the case, for example, in the story 'How do we manage Samiya's public sexualised behaviours?' in which 'Emily,' a middle leader within a special school, reflects on how she is ultimately 'really glad that I got to be her (Samiya's) teacher'.

One of the dilemmas within the typology of 'Four Dilemmas for Inclusive Practice', outlined in Figure 9.1, is the Dilemma of Possibility. Through this dilemma, teachers interact with their doubts around what is feasible in relation to inclusive practice, and what they are capable of. It is a dilemma that 'Natasha' would have inevitably needed to overcome in the story 'How do I ensure that pupils from the Area Resource Base experience the wonder of Science?'. In this story, Natasha takes the courageous step of moving her lessons with the learners from the unit for learners with complex learning difficulties, which is attached to the secondary school where she teaches Science, and where she is timetabled to work with several times a week, to a lab. The Dilemma of Possibility is also a dilemma that was grappled with by Polly in the story 'Should I be having this conversation about death?' in which she wonders about her capacity, as a teacher, to explore sensitive issues with her learners with SLD. The analysis of the stories suggests that teacher wellbeing is integral to any interaction with this dilemma.

Feeling Connected to, and Collaborating with Others

The analysis of the stories suggested that granting professional agency to teachers does not require them to necessarily make decisions alone, or for them to be at liberty to take irresponsible risks, without their decision-making being moderated by others. Instead, a commitment to teacher agency is coupled with a commitment to depart from the individualism in education described by Sachs (2000) by adopting 'new ways of working' (p. 82) that resist it, that involve collaboration with others. As shown in Figure 9.2, this is one of the various ways in which each of the 'essences' of 'inclusive practice with learners with SPMLD and/or at risk of exclusion,' that were found through the analysis of the 'dilemma stories' are interconnected.

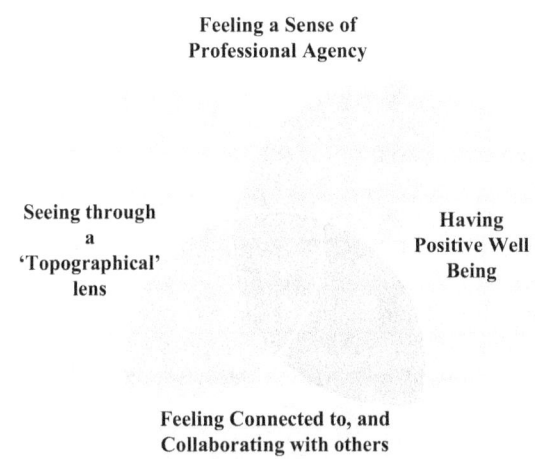

Figure 9.2 Interconnections between the essences of inclusive practice with learners with SPMLD and/or at risk of exclusion.

In total, this analysis found four distinct essences of the phenomenon of 'inclusive practice with learners at risk of exclusion and/or with SPMLD.' Although distinct, the identified essence of 'feeling connected to and collaborating with others,' is closely entwined with the other three, as highlighted by the particular stories discussed in this section. Out of the stories analysed in this study, 26 involved close professional collaboration in relation to learners with SPMLD and/or at risk of exclusion. This included collaboration between teachers, between teaching and non-teaching staff, and between teachers and wider professionals such as health visitors. It also highlighted collaboration, which may not have been possible without educators being granted professional agency, without them having a sense of wellbeing, and without them adopting a 'topographical' approach to teaching.

The story 'How do we ensure that the learning of our pupils with Severe Learning Difficulties are being fully supported in RE lessons?' for example, suggests that meaningful collaboration in education involves embracing your own professional agency as a practitioner, alongside promoting the professional agency of others. In this story, Polly, as the head of department for RE, puts systems in place, which focus teaching assistants (TAs) on the assessment and evaluation of learning in a lesson. This effectively enables them to make reasoned judgements with some autonomy, rather than merely see their role as ensuring that learners complete tasks, regardless of whether-or-not they have actually learnt anything:

Setting up the unit awards was one way of preventing the TAs from completing the work that had been set for learners themselves, which often happened. They would be in the room saying 'I've done it! Finished!' and I would be thinking 'We're only 10 minutes into the lesson!'... The Unit Awards have a level of accountability for the TAs. At the end of lessons, they have to fill in an observation box and reach judgements about the skills they had observed learners doing.

Polly's experience in another story 'Should I be accepting the argument "all teachers are teachers of SEND" when I don't find the SEND Department of my school particularly helpful?' provides further insight into effective professional collaboration. There is irony, for example, in how the statement 'all teachers are teachers are SEND,' which emphasises shared responsibility for learners, is effectively used by a SEND department in this story, to resist an invitation from a teacher to collaborate.

For Polly, teachers within the SEND department within her school 'have been trained in the old system and therefore sticking to that system.' Instead, she would like them to provide leadership and build capacity for inclusion across the school. However, she finds that they are instead focussed on the input which they give within the on-site specialist unit, whenever pupils with SEND are withdrawn from mainstream classes. Although Polly did not disagree with the assertion that 'all teachers are teachers with SEND,' she felt like the dialogue had been shut down when this was said to her by her colleagues in the SEND department, and that she was being perceived as someone who was cynically trying to get the pupil removed from her class.

Broadly speaking, Polly, in her story, is committed to the principle of 'all teachers' being 'teachers of SEND.' It is principle that is emphasised in the 2014 SEND Code of Practice (Department for Education and Department for Health, 2014), representing a welcome move away from any older models and approaches in which only 'SEND teachers' were seen to be capable of working with 'SEND learners.' However, for Polly, the term 'all teachers are teachers of SEND' had been weaponised by the SEND department within her school, leading to a situation where 'as subject teachers we're sort of left to our own devices' without a coherent strategy for supporting pupils. Polly is therefore torn. She wants to build the capacity of teachers within the RE department she leads, to be 'teachers of SEND.' However, she sees this as only possible if the SEND department adopts a 'newer,' more strategic role, rather than retreat back into the 'older' ways of doing things separately from the rest of the school.

Very powerfully, Polly's story serves to highlight how 'all teachers' are being 'teachers of SEND' is something that does not become a reality by merely saying it. It suggests that teachers need empowerment, agency, and dialogue with others, which resists the individualism in education that Sachs (2000) associates with a culture of 'Managerial Professionalism.' It was such individualism that seemed to be reflected in the model of SEND provision in Polly's story, in which a separate SEND department focussed on separate input in separate spaces that ultimately separated colleagues.

Valuing collaborative problem-solving in education, and challenging individualism, arguably has implications for how we might deliver initial teacher training. If we view teaching as a collective endeavour, then we are less likely to advocate for routes into the profession, through which individual teachers become individually qualified to individually work with particular SEND categories or labels. If we emphasise how all teachers have a collective responsibility to all children, then we do not need to focus on nurturing 'expertise' in SLD or PMLD (e.g., through SEN-specific teaching qualifications). Instead, we need to focus on routes into teaching that effectively develop more universal qualities for educating all learners, such as those for being part of a professional learning community and for interacting with a diverse range of perspectives on the issues impacting each unique young person or child. We also need to focus on routes into teaching which enhance the capacity of educators to implement the 'topographical' approaches that were found within the teachers' 'dilemma stories' and are outlined below.

Seeing through a 'Topographical' Lens

In Geology and Art History, the term 'topography' broadly refers to the arrangement of the forms and features of an area, for example, through maps or landscape paintings (Lorek and Medyńska-Gulij, 2020). It is a term that could be used metaphorically, to capture an important 'essence' of inclusive practice with learners with SPMLD and/or at risk of exclusion, that was arrived at through the analysis of the teachers' 'dilemma stories.'

In the same way as a topographical artist or cartographer closely studies the environment they are representing, the topographical teacher is a student of their particular pupils and co-constructs learning experiences based on what has been learnt about them through close observation and formative assessment. Extending the metaphor of 'topography,' Table 9.1 outlines the practices of 'The Topographical Artist,' 'The Topographical Cartographer,' and 'The Topographical Teacher' alongside each other.

Across the stories analysed for the research study, there are numerous exemplifications of this notion of 'Topographical Teaching.' In the story 'What does inclusion look like for a learner with complex medical needs, who is self-isolating?', for example, the decisions of 'Emily,' relating to the use of specific technologies in the special school in which she is a middle leader, could be viewed as being informed by a topographical pedagogical approach. It is a story in which Emily had the option of using a 'robot' device to connect her class with her pupil, 'Leo,' who was learning away from the others, in a separate room, in the aftermath of the lockdowns associated with the

Table 9.1 An overview of 'topographical' practices in art, cartography, and education

	The Topographical Artist	The Topographical Cartographer	The Topographical Teacher
Observation	Carefully observes a landscape to create a valid representation of it	Observes and captures the objective features of a landscape (e.g., through photographs and sketches) to enable an accurate representation of a place on a map	Observes learner responses to teaching to inform ongoing and iterative planning
Capturing	Captures geological features of a place, such as terrain, vegetation, and weather conditions	Takes appropriate measurements to ensure that physical features are represented accurately on a map and that terrain can be explored and navigated safely. Requires skills in representing and reading information on topographical maps	Uses formative and summative assessment to gain insight into their learners and effectively elicit misconceptions, barriers to learning, and/or effective strategies
Considering 'the Bigger Picture'	Contextualises any human or animal subjects within the broader landscape they are situated within	Explores what is beneath the surface of the land, to represent geological features on a map that are not immediately observable	Considers the 'bigger picture' beyond the immediate lesson or upcoming assessment; What are the learner's aspirations? How can they be best prepared now for where they intend to be in several years' time?
Engaging with Reality	Is grounded in realism and largely bases its work on observed realities, rather than on the content of its imagination	Creates a map that is highly informative and offers insight into a terrain	Teaches the actual learners within their classroom rather than fictional ones that are imagined in relation to diagnoses or perceived ability groups

(Continued)

Table 9.1 (Continued)

	The Topographical Artist	The Topographical Cartographer	The Topographical Teacher
Being Responsive	Responds to the sublime and/or untamed dimension to the natural world (Burke, 2014)	Captures changes to terrain through updating maps, Considers how factors such as coastal erosion or tectonic activity have changed the terrain, to inform updates	Pays attention to topographical shifts within their classroom and adapts their practice accordingly. What seems to be 'working' may be ineffective the next
Being Creative	Channels their personal creativity to represent landscapes from their unique perspective, to create an original piece of artwork	Is continually making creative decisions on how to communicate complex information clearly Requires skills in representing and reading information on topographical maps	Shape their own inclusive practice creatively rather than follow a pre-defined formula

Edwards, T. (2025). Topographical teaching: A metaphor for professional practice with learners with severe, profound, and multiple learning difficulties. *Impact* 23. This table was originally published by Chartered College, in the online version of the 'Impact' journal and is available at: https://my.chartered.college/impact_article/topographical-teaching-a-metaphor-for-professional-practice-with-learners-with-severe-profound-and-multiple-learning-difficulties/.

Covid-19 pandemic. The technology was in place within her school for her to place this robot in her classroom to represent Leo, and for this to enable him to see and hear everything going on in the classroom through a connection between the robot and a device in a separate room where his learning was located. Although using the robot was regarded as innovative and exciting, Emily reached the conclusion that the non-glamorous use of basic video-conferencing software using iPads was more effective in enabling Leo's authentic inclusion.

Another exemplification of the notion of 'Topographical Teaching' can be found in the story 'How should we be assessing the learning and progress of learners within our special school?' in which 'Joanne,' a deputy head teacher, explains a change in approach to assessment, which reflects a commitment to capturing an 'authentic picture' of learning and progress, rather than a distorted one, which merely gives an appearance of progress. In the below extract from this story, Joanne describes the 'old' system of assessment that the school had decided to abandon:

> There were lots of things about what we were doing before that weren't sitting right. We had been using this commercial software package to assess our pupils. It was one of those online things where teachers had to click on a box for each standard that a pupil had achieved, and then it calculated what level they were on. This did not provide an authentic picture of learning across the school. For example, there were teachers who tried to be really honest with their reporting. Their learners were shown to not be making any progress because not enough boxes within the system had been ticked. This was often in spite of us knowing that the pupil had made enormous progress with us, which was frustrating.
>
> There were also those teachers that saw that the algorithm said that that child had to make three points of progress, so they over-supported the child to produce those three pieces of work that they would need to tick a particular box. The system then 'showed' that 'progress' had been made, but it was not authentic.

This 'old' system of assessment, which Joanne and her colleagues decided to move away from, was far from being 'topographical.' Under this old system, educators were not meaningfully interacting with the landscape of their classroom, and generated assessment information that reflected fantasy rather than reality. The approach associated with this old system also focussed teachers on demonstrating progress in the short term. As the above quote from Joanne's story shows, this led to practices such as 'over-supporting' pupils with particular tasks, to enable a box to be ticked, in ways that most likely disregarded the 'bigger picture' of longer-term, more sustainable learning and development. To adopt 'Topographical Teaching,' educators must consider this 'bigger picture' in the same way as topographical cartographers would consider the contours and creeks beyond the surface of a terrain, which are not immediately visible.

In policy dialogues relating to education, health, and care planning for young people with SPMLD beyond the age of 18, the notion of 'Topographical Teaching' has a possible role to play in highlighting the value of education, delivered by teachers with skills in formative assessment and responsive planning. As highlighted within another story that was analysed for the research study, 'If they're making beans and toast with us, are they learning?', viewing holistic developmental goals as distinct from academic ones can mean that provision for learners with SPMLD runs the risk of no longer being seen to require input from 'education.' This can lead to local authorities withdrawing funding for specialist colleges for older learners with SPMLD, making the argument that it represents greater value for money to place them in a social care setting, rather than an education one. The analysis of the stories suggests, however, that it is most likely a topographical mindset, within the domain of education, that supports progress and development towards holistic goals for young people with SPMLD, thus strengthening the arguments for funding their continuing education.

With topographical art, two separate illustrators may create sketches of the exact same place that, whilst sharing essential characteristics, differ enormously. Similarly, Topographical Teaching seems to involve teachers being empowered to shape their practice in unique ways, according to their interpretations. The role of realism to topography is evident in the essential similarities between any two paintings of the same place, completed at around the same time, which depict objective features of a landscape that the two painters are unable to deny. However, both paintings also serve as a reminder that no two artists will ever create exactly the same picture, independently from one another, and that individual creativity brings something to each unique representation. Although there are many objective ways in which practice can be unhelpful to children and young people, there are also many ways in which practice can be the opposite. Rather than perceive any singular 'correct' way of implementing inclusive practice, therefore, the notion of 'Topographical Teaching' serves to emphasise that there are vast, if not infinite, possibilities.

References

Booth, T., & Ainscow, M. (2002). Index for inclusion developing learning and participation in schools: Editing and production for CSIE Mark Vaughan. *Restoration Ecology*, 15(2002).
Burke, E. (2014). *A philosophical enquiry into the origin of our ideas of the sublime and beautiful: With an introductory discourse concerning taste and several other additions.* Cambridge University Press. (Cambridge Library Collection)
Edwards, T. (2025). Beyond the 'dilemma of difference': An analysis of stories from experienced teachers about their inclusive practice. *British Educational Research Journal*, 51, 1421–1444. https://doi.org/10.1002/berj.4129
Florian, L., & Beaton, M. (2018). Inclusive pedagogy in action: Getting it right for every child. *International Journal of Inclusive Education*, 22(8). https://doi.org/10.1080/13603116.2017.1412513
Lorek, D., & Medyńska-Gulij, B. (2020). Scope of information in the legends of topographical maps in the nineteenth century–Urmesstischblätter. *Cartographic Journal*, 57(2). https://doi.org/10.1080/00087041.2018.1547471
Merleau-Ponty, M. (2013). Phenomenology of perception. In *Phenomenology of Perception*. London: Routledge. https://doi.org/10.4324/9780203720714
Norwich, B. (2008). Dilemmas of difference, inclusion and disability: International perspectives on placement. *European Journal of Special Needs Education*, 23(4). https://doi.org/10.1080/08856250802387166
Norwich, B. (2010). Dilemmas of difference, curriculum and disability: International perspectives. *Comparative Education*, 46(2). https://doi.org/10.1080/03050061003775330
Sachs, J. (2000). The activist professional. *Journal of Educational Change*, 1, 77–94.
Schon, D. A. (1991). *The Reflective Practitioner: How Professionals Think in Action.* New York, NY: Basic Books.
Standards and Testing Agency. (2024, 15 April). *Guidance: The engagement model.* https://www.Gov.Uk/Government/Publications/the-Engagement-Model/the-Engagement-Model
van Manen, M. (2016). Phenomenology of practice. In *Phenomenology of Practice*. New York, NY: Routledge. https://doi.org/10.4324/9781315422657

Chapter 10

Dilemma-based professional learning

For any teacher who has remained in the profession for decades, wherever they are in the world, the profile of the learners they have encountered is likely to have changed over the years, and the prevalence of particular diagnoses and labels is likely to be very different now from what it was when they entered the profession. They may also have found that terms such as 'Severe Learning Difficulties' have been used and applied differently, in different schools that they have worked in at around the same time, as well as at different points in their career history. This requires them to rethink strategies that may have previously been generally effective within their classroom, and to navigate unanticipated situations which they are unlikely to have been directly prepared for, as part of their initial teacher training. Such changing realities also emphasise the inevitability of professional dilemmas and the value of continuing professional development, which enhances the capacity of teachers to respond to them. In unanticipated situations, where knowledge from previous training and development activities may not be directly applicable, teachers need values and skills for interpretation and decision-making, and these need to be iteratively developed through access to high-quality, continual professional development.

This chapter explores a range of approaches to the professional learning of educators, which are 'dilemma-based' and focus on the development of 'Craft knowledge,' as a resource for supporting classroom practitioners to reach decisions, particularly in situations in which they are required to 'make a choice between two alternatives where neither is favourable' (Norwich, 2010, p. 117).

Teacher Education, Inclusive Practice, and 'Craft Knowledge'

The notion of 'Craft knowledge' has been written about extensively, in academic literature related to initial teacher education (Hagger and McIntyre, 2006), the continuing professional development of educators (Tripp, 2012), and on the principle of Inclusive Pedagogy (e.g., Black-Hawkins and Florian, 2012). It is a notion that is largely associated with the work of Hagger and

McIntyre (2006) who define Craft knowledge as 'all the complex, largely tacit knowledge that informs the contextualised professional judgements made by individual teachers in their everyday practice' (p. 34). The term 'Craft knowledge,' therefore, does not relate directly to knowledge of teaching techniques or the 'Craft' of teaching. It relates instead to 'practical wisdom' (Florian and Beaton, 2018, p. 873) and has similarities with the Aristotelian notion of *phronesis*, which is making sense of situations, and translating them into decisions around a response or course of action.

Craft knowledge is distinguishable from other forms of knowledge for working in a classroom, including 'specialist knowledge' for working with particular Special Educational Needs and Disabilities (SEND) or 'subject knowledge' around the actual content of the curriculum being taught. It therefore arguably has a unique role to play in strengthening inclusive practice in education, which tends to be associated with the navigation of professional dilemmas, within situations in which other forms of knowledge cannot necessarily be utilised directly (e.g. Florian, 2010 p. 62; Paulsrud, 2024). If we are to assume that the same action within a classroom is simultaneously inclusive and exclusive, rather than either one or the other, as is emphasised across the research literature on Inclusive Pedagogy (e.g., Black-Hawkins and Florian 2012, p. 568), then Craft knowledge logically has a role to play for teachers in navigating ambiguity.

In the subsequent sections of this chapter, a range of dilemma-based approaches to teacher development will be outlined. These approaches serve as frameworks to develop the Craft knowledge of teachers, through a positive exploration of professional dilemmas. The approaches outlined in the subsequent sections of this chapter will be as follows:

1. Lesson Study
2. Learning Study
3. Critical Incident Analysis
4. Dilemma-Based Coaching
5. Philosophy for Teacher Education

In outlining the above five approaches, their scope for developing the capacity of teachers in relation to learners with SPMLD will be explored. Although these five approaches do by no means reflect the entirety of ways in which teachers can develop their Craft knowledge, as a resource for negotiating professional dilemmas, they represent a variety of different tools that are likely to suit a range of different contexts where SPMLD learners are taught.

Approach One: Lesson Study

Lesson Study is an approach to collaboratively planning, observing, and reflecting on lessons (Dudley, 2014a, 2014b). Its origins have been traced to

Chinese Confucianism (Dudley, 2014a) and its development in Japan over a century ago (Norwich et al. 2021). In its UK form, Lesson Study typically involves following a cycle(s) through which a 'Lesson Study Group' of between two and five teachers, engage in joint lesson observations based on focus pupils, follow-up post-observation dialogues, and the planning of a subsequent lesson (often taught by another teacher in the group) which is also observed and reflected upon (Dudley, 2014b). There are published writings on lesson studies that have taken place amongst teachers from within the same school (Edwards, 2021) and across different schools (e.g., Dudley et al. 2019). Lesson Studies between teachers and wider educational professionals, such as educational psychologists, have also been published (Norwich et al., 2016).

For Norwich, Benham-Clarke and Goei (2021) 'Lesson Study and Lesson Study-related professional development practices embody the values of inclusive teaching and reflective practice' (p. 309). The essential features of Lesson Study (LS) allow teachers to engage in co-operative problem-solving processes, to address barriers to learning that pupils bring with them into classrooms. One example of this is in an area-wide LS, focussed on teaching Mathematics, in which participating teachers gained insight into ways to support learners presenting with a fear of the subject (Dudley et al., 2019, p. 209).

At the University of Exeter in the United Kingdom, Norwich (Norwich, 2014) developed materials on using LS in the assessment and identification of pupils with SEND, which can be applied to learners with SPMLD. These materials include case studies of how lesson studies have provided classroom practitioners with valuable insight into 'case pupils.' One case study, for example, involved an LS centred around a 15-year-old young man with Down Syndrome. Through the process of LS, his teacher, and the teaching assistant working with him, started to recognise how they stepped in too quickly during lessons and offered help too early. They also established that too many instructions were being directed at him at the same time, and that he often arrived at a lesson, having forgotten what he had learnt in the lesson before. One of the teachers participating in this LS commented that the 'collaborative working with two other colleagues was invaluable for me.' Another teacher-reflection from this LS commented 'it has helped me to understand his needs in depth and make changes to teaching to address these needs' (p. 39).

In some iterations of the approach, a 'Lesson Study Cycle' also involves interviews with pupils in which they provide feedback on what enabled them to succeed (or otherwise) in a lesson. For a 'LS' involving the teaching of learners with SPMLD, there are multiple barriers to such interviews being a positive or meaningful experience for pupils, or to it being feasible to conduct them with any authenticity. Learners, for example, may not have any spoken language. When asked to choose a photograph of their favourite part of a baking session, they may not be able to make the connection between a photographic image of them rolling cookie dough and the moment in which they were doing this in reality. In fact, with learners with SPMLD, any activity for eliciting their feelings and opinions on a lesson could in fact be the focus for a LS in itself, with there inevitably being a considerable amount for educators to reflect upon and interpret.

To place the 'voice' of learners with SPMLD at the centre of a LS, therefore, the process is likely to benefit from tools such as the Engagement Model, which was published by the Department for Education for England and Wales in 2019. It is a model that is closely based on research led by Carpenter et al. (2011) and the initial development of the Engagement Profile and Scale. Both the Engagement Model and its earlier iteration of the Engagement Profile and Scale focus educators on strengthening the overall 'engagement' of learners with complex barriers to learning, who are working significantly below age expectations. Using the Engagement Model, educators observe the responses of learners, which are often likely to be very subtle, and identify moments where these learners were giving indications of capacity in relation to five 'engagement indicators.' These engagement indicators include 'Exploration,' 'Realisation,' 'Anticipation,' 'Persistence,' and 'Initiation.'

A cycle for a hypothetical 'LS,' centred around the telling of a particular sensory story called 'The Queen in the Garden,' is outlined in Figure 10.1.

The ways in which the Engagement Model might support a hypothetical LS, based on the sensory story 'The Queen in the Garden' are outlined in Table 10.1. On this table, under the heading from the Engagement Model, 'Anticipation' for example, it is noted that 'Katie' sticks out her tongue, at the point where there is some buzzing of bees (after having enjoyed the story before, on seven separate occasions), just before the point where the learners are able to opt to have a taste of some honey. Under the heading 'Persistence,'

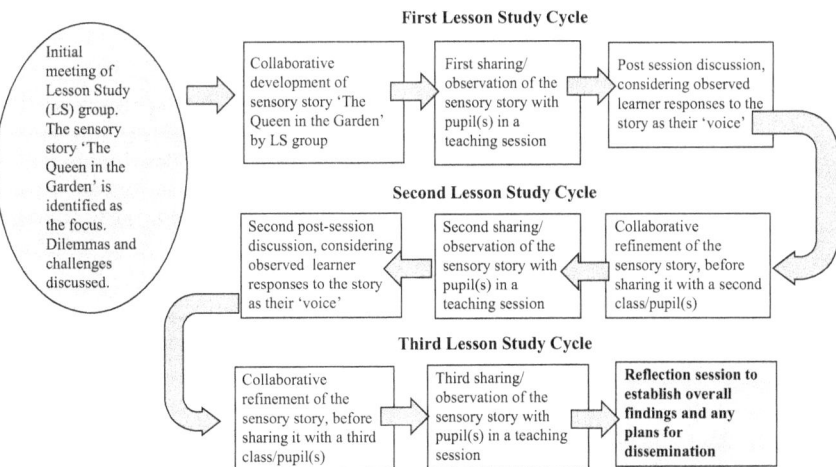

Figure 10.1 Process for a Lesson Study, centred around the hypothetical sensory story 'The Queen in the Garden.' (Adapted from the Lesson Study process outlined by Dudley, 2014a, 2014b)

118 Severe, Profound and Multiple Learning Difficulties in School

Table 10.1 Using the Engagement Model to make notes of Katie's responses to the sensory story 'The Queen in the Garden' as part of a Lesson Study

LESSON STUDY OBSERVATION PROFORMA
Teacher: YE   **Class Team**: BN, HU, YE.   **Observers(s)**: PY
Focus of Lesson Study: 'The Queen in the Garden' Sensory Story (Topic: Plants and Flowers)
Focus Learner: Katie (Year 5, PMLD)

	Question for observers*	**Observation notes**	**Next Steps**
Exploration	Is the learner building on their 'initial reaction to a new stimulus or activity'?	Katie explores the tray of leaves with her feet	Hide toy caterpillars in leaves for learners to find
Realisation	Is the learner finding out new things about the stimulus (and responding accordingly)?		Could learners have the opportunity to use iPads to control the volume of bees buzzing and music?
Anticipation	Is the learner expecting something to happen, based on previous experience?	Katie sticks out her tongue when she hears the buzzing of the bees, to taste the honey?	
Persistence	Is the learner sustaining attention and/or showing 'a determined effort to interact with the stimulus or activity'?	Katie stretches to reach for the velvet material	Could the velvet material be moved even further away, to further develop persistence?
Initiation	Is the learner investigating 'a stimulus or activity, to bring about a desired outcome'?	Katie grabs the toy bird after seeing Rochelle squeeze it, to make it 'tweet'	Making the 'tweet' sound requires requisite fine motor skills. Could learners be encouraged to tap the bird to prompt the adult to squeeze it?

* Wording based on guidance from Standards and Testing Agency (2024)

a note is made of how Katie continues to stretch until she can reach the velvet material that represents the Queen's robes. Through following the 'LS' cycle in Figure 10.1, the 'Lesson Study Group' can then enter into a discussion around dilemmas associated with this particular sensory story. To what extent should practitioners persist with developing learners' persistence in relation to reaching the velvet material? At what point does having the material they may want to grab, some distance away from them, become over-harsh and counter-productive? How do we know that learners, who are pre-verbal, are consenting to having a taste of the honey? What should we look for, when reading this story, to also ensure that no individual learner is assumed to be non-consenting (to tasting the honey) when they would actually like some?

In relation to learners with SPMLD, there is also a strong argument, however, that it is impossible to replicate a session, or 'lesson,' developed for one group of learners, to optimise it for delivery to another. Refinements to the telling of the sensory story 'The Queen and the Garden,' therefore, making observations of 'Katie's' responses, using the engagement indicators within the 'Engagement Model,' may optimise the experience of the story, but quite possibly only for Katie. Other learners with SPMLD, due to their particular unique learning profiles, are likely to benefit from very different refinements. Rather than the 'collaborative development of a lesson' (Elliott, 2009, p. 4) there is an argument that the focus of practitioner enquiry should be on expanding the range of strategies or tools which practitioners can draw upon when supporting learners to reach learning goals across a more extended period of time.

Approach Two: Learning Study

In addition to 'LS,' the associated approach of 'Learning Study' offers a framework for enabling the development of 'Craft knowledge' through the navigation of professional dilemmas. Rather than focus on the 'collaborative development of a lesson' (Elliott, 2009, p. 4), Learning Study tends to look more broadly at sequences of teaching and the curriculum that is being offered to learners, over time (Ling Lo, 2012). In particular parts of the world, including at the University of Gothenburg in Sweden, Learning Study has been developed as an approach to supporting the professional learning of teachers (e.g., Innabi and Emanuelsson, 2021; Magnusson et al., 2021).

Due to its underpinning theoretical foundations in phenomenography. 'Learning Study' offers something distinct, to the development of teachers, which can be applied to the enhancement of their inclusive practice. The term 'phenomenography' refers to the study of, and the (mis)conceptions which are held in relation to, a phenomenon or an 'object of learning' (Ling Lo 2012, p. 16) that is being taught. Examples of 'objects of learning' for mainstream secondary school contexts, might include developing an accurate understanding of how the human eye works, as explored in a phenomenographic study by Marton (1981). For learners with SPMLD, possible 'objects of learning' can be found, for example, in the 'Routes for Learning' materials which form part of the national curriculum for Wales (Welsh Government, 2025). These materials include a 'Route Map' which outlines broader goals around developmental milestones that an individual with SPMLD might be working on, such as that of maintaining 'joint attention' on something with others.

According to Donovan (1999, in Ling Lo, 2012, p. 13), learners bring a range of (mis)conceptions to the classroom, in relation to any object of learning, which teachers must interact with. If we were to apply this point to learners with SPMLD, working at a pre-intentional level, where a focus on misconceptions would not be appropriate, we could alternatively highlight the range of barriers that these learners bring to any learning encounter. From a phenomenographic perspective, therefore, the task of the educator of learners with SPMLD would be to interact with these barriers to facilitate learning around more developmental 'objects of learning.' The approach of Learning Study can be utilised to enable such interaction.

Learning Study also has a basis in 'variation theory,' which is the idea that learners often need to be exposed to multiple representations of a phenomenon in order to truly comprehend the essence of it. In explaining this, Ling Lo (2012) uses the example of triangles. In order to understand what a triangle is (or isn't), a learner needs to be exposed to different types of triangles, triangles of different colours, and of different sizes. It is through Learning Study that teachers can extend the variation that is offered to learners, and the 'ways in' to understanding, that can be employed to support any struggling pupils. This has been found to be a valuable tool for supporting professional development in inclusive education settings, transforming teachers into 'phenomenographic explorers,' exploring and responding to the (mis)conceptions (or barriers) of their pupils (Edwards, 2021, p. 127).

A possible cycle for conducting a 'Learning Study,' focussed on learners with SPMLD, can be found in Figure 10.2. This is a cycle which engages practitioners in a phenomenographic exploration of the barriers that learners with SPMLD will bring, to making progress around more developmental, or holistic, 'objects of learning.' It is also a cycle through which practitioners can consider dilemmas associated with this. The cycle begins and ends with a session, with a lead researcher/facilitator.

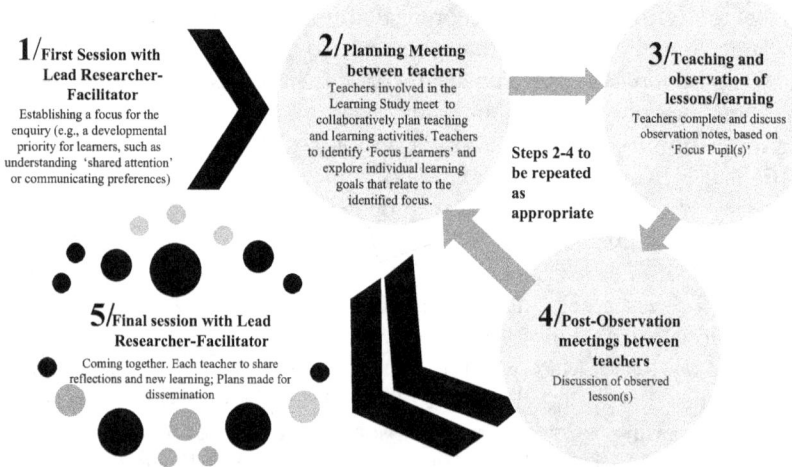

Figure 10.2 Process for a 'Learning Study' for education settings with learners with SPMLD.

- The session at the beginning is to establish a focus for the 'Learning Study,' and possibly introduce a research article, or a particular insight from neuroscience, or a pedagogical approach that educators may not yet be aware of, that could provide a basis for the ongoing enquiry.
- The subsequent stages of the cycle involve educators coming together to jointly plan, observe each other teach, and reflect with one another, during post-observation meetings. This 'Learning Study Cycle' is in many ways identical to any cycle for conducting a 'LS.' However, its emphasis is on developing practitioners to support pupils in relation to 'objects of learning' over time, rather than on perfecting a lesson so that it is more effective the next time it is taught.
- The final session in the cycle is to enable 'reflection-on-action,' (Schon, 1991) and capture any new learning that comes from this, and provide a safe space for educators to simultaneously articulate their 'Craft knowledge,' and develop it.

In the previous section of this chapter, on LS, the Engagement Model was cited as an example of a potentially valuable tool for focussing professional conversations around the teaching and learning of those with SPMLD. This model is based on the assumption that maximising engagement is an overall aim of education for those with complex barriers to participation. Although the 'Engagement Model' serves as a potentially valuable tool for enhancing a 'LS' or 'Learning Study' focussed on learners with SPMLD, it is not the only available tool. A range of other approaches can support educators to assess and evaluate the participation of learners with SPMLD in a session, elicit 'voice,' and establish next steps for developing practice. Hart's Ladder of Participation (1992), for example, has an established place in the history of thinking about children's participation. As shown in Table 10.2, this ladder outlines a set of 'rungs' which we move up, the more authentically and meaningfully children are participating and being actively involved in decision-making.

In a 'Learning Study,' the rungs of Hart's ladder could be used to explore the level of agency and autonomy which learners with SPMLD are granted within an activity or teaching session. For this purpose, more recent adaptations of Hart's Ladder of Participation may also be helpful (Dolaty, Tait, and Brunskill, 2022). Whereas Hart's ladder can be criticised for being too linear or hierarchical, for example, the alternative 'Degrees of Participation' model (Treseder, 1997), which is based on it, represents each form of participation alongside one another, on a wheel. This is due to a recognition that the extent of an individual's participation is likely to vary between different days and between different points within the same day (and indeed at different moments within the same session!). It is a recognition that therefore has coherence with looking at learning and participation over time, as part of a Learning Study. An adaptation of Treseder's model, for education settings with SPMLD learners, is outlined in Figure 10.3.

122 Severe, Profound and Multiple Learning Difficulties in School

Table 10.2 Using Hart's Ladder of Participation to explore the participation of learners with SPMLD in schools

Rung	State of Children's Participation	What this might look like with SPMLD learners in schools
8	Decision-making is child-centred and shared with adults	Adults leave sufficient time to wait for responses from learners.
7	What is happening is child-initiated	Responses from learners (e.g., to a sensory story) are discussed and reflected upon. Different possible interpretations of these responses are explored, supported by formative assessment.
6	What is happening is adult-initiated, but decisions are shared with children	Resources to support communication (for example) are bespoke to individuals, reflecting preferences and interests.
5	Children are consulted and informed	Activities may be adult-initiated and led but pace may be determined by the responses of the child, and their state of wellbeing on a particular day.
4	Children are assigned, but informed	
3	Tokenism	Activities that are alleged to promote participation are staged. For example, a learner may be deemed to have made a choice by selecting between two photographs, when the reality is that they haven't. They may be presented as participating in a school play, when they are merely placed on stage for the purposes of 'showing' the community that they are being 'included.'
2	Decoration	
1	Manipulation	

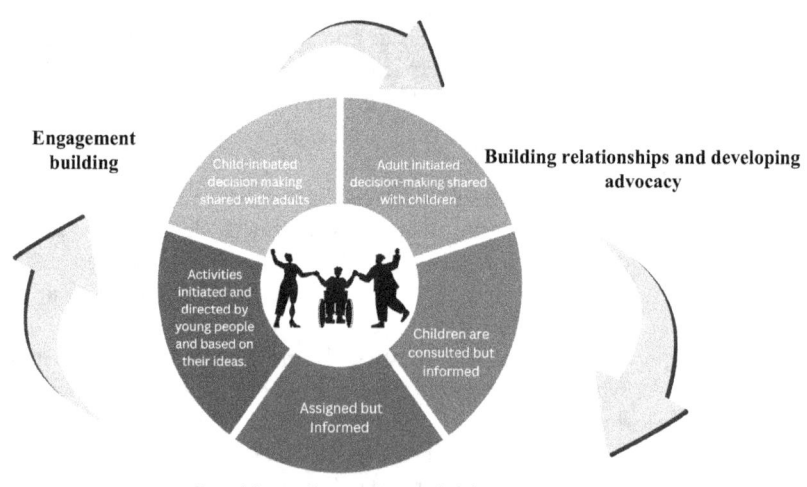

Figure 10.3 A model of participation to support professional dialogues in education settings with learners with SPMLD. (Adapted from Treseder's 1997 'Wheel of Participation')

Approach Three: Critical Incident Analysis

Professional learning using 'Critical Incidents in Teaching' (Tripp, 2012) is another possible approach for developing inclusive classroom practitioners who can respond to the diversity within their classroom. For Tripp, a 'critical incident' is a moment within a career that has prompted a rethink of existing practices and/or ways of viewing things. Critical incidents tend not to be 'dramatic or obvious' (Tripp 2012, p. 24) and 'occur within routine practice' (p. 25). They are 'critical' due to the way in which they are analysed. Rather than being focussed on any practical or technical dimension to a teacher's thinking, they may uncover hidden biases, rooted in social conventions, or give insight into lived experiences or perspectives which challenge existing assumptions and world views.

Examples of critical incidents involving learners with SPMLD can be found across the 'dilemma stories' that were collected for the research study, on which this book is largely based. One of these critical incidents is in the story 'How do we manage Samiya's public sexualised behaviours?' in which 'Emily,' a teacher within a special school, explores the preconceived ideas she had initially held, which led to an incorrect hypothesis around the underlying cause of her pupil's actions. Whereas Emily, along with her colleagues, assumed Samiya's seemingly sexualised behaviours to be self-stimulatory, they were most likely due to the urinary infection she eventually tested positive for.

Emily's 'critical incident' within this story raises further considerations around the principle of 'age-appropriateness' in relation to teenagers with SEND, which pervades much of the literature (Forster, 2010). Whilst it remains a moral imperative not to infantilise individuals with SLD approaching adulthood, this incident emphasised how an uncritical insistence on 'age-appropriateness' can possibly cause us, for example, to link behaviours to puberty and/or make assumptions that are 'inappropriate' to the person or situation. In Figure 10.4, 'Emily's' story about Samiya is dissected using Tripp's (2012) framework for the analysis of critical incidents (p. 26).

For Tripp, teachers need to be 'intellectually expert about expert practice' (p. 5). He argued that this is supported by asking evaluative questions about teaching, such as 'What else could I have done better?' and by drawing upon 'common wisdom.' For Tripp, Craft knowledge plays a role in the formulation, interpretation, and analysis of critical incidents by teachers, and in any transformations in practice that result from them (pp. 6–7).

Approach Four: Dilemma-Based Coaching

There is a vast array of models, research studies, and policy debates related to the use of coaching as a professional development tool. One model that is dominant within this array is that of 'instructional coaching' (Knight, 2007, Knight et al., 2016). This is a form of coaching through which a more experienced or proficient practitioner guides a more novice educator through the

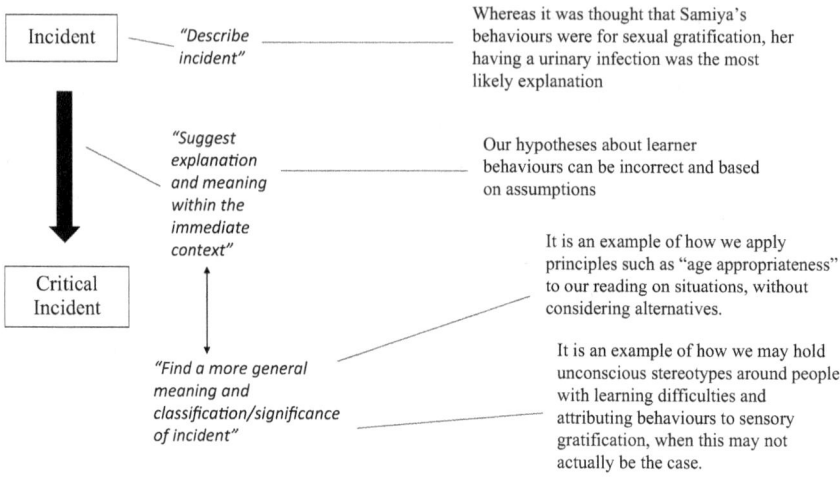

Figure 10.4 Applying the steps outlined by Tripp (2012, p. 26) to the analysis of a 'critical incident,' involving a learner with SLD, in Emily's story.

adoption of specific evidence-based strategies, such as those related to behaviour management or the teaching of reading through systematic synthetic phonics. Through instructional coaching, technical aspects of classroom practice can be analysed, and adjustments can be suggested by the more experienced coach. Such adjustments are likely to have closer fidelity to the particular pedagogical approaches or strategies being implemented. In settings where there are learners with SPMLD, instructional coaching might be considered an appropriate method for developing an educator to deliver a methodology such as 'Attention Autism' (Davies, 2025) through which sessions follow a defined sequence of stages, to maximise the engagement of learners and the overall development of shared attention. Another example of where instructional coaching might be considered appropriate in settings with learners with SPMLD might be in relation to a picture-exchange communication system (PECS) and the routines associated with it.

Whilst serving as a framework for ensuring that learners in classrooms are benefitting from approaches that have a basis in research evidence, there are many more available coaching models for developing teachers. A wide range of approaches to coaching in education exist, which enable educators to explore the dilemmas inherent in their practice (e.g., Pask and Joy, 2007). These approaches offer various coaching cycles and methods of questioning that support the processes of 'reflection-on-action' and 'reflection-in-action' outlined by Schon (1991). As well as the coaching (Schon, 1991, pp. 76–104) itself, practitioners are also having what Schon referred to as a 'conversation with the situation' underpinning the dilemma that is the focus of professional discussion. When effective, this may enable practitioners to rethink their initial impressions of a situation and start to see things in new ways. Through this, they may further develop their 'Craft knowledge,' as well as their professional values. The impact of this may arguably not be as immediately obvious as that of instructional coaching, which may make rapid and tangible improvements to more precise and observable teaching skills. However, there is also the argument that enhanced technical skills for teaching are not the only, or most desirable, positive outcome of coaching in education.

According to Shulman (2007), developing professional practice involves an apprenticeship of 'the head,' 'the heart,' and 'the hand.' Learning a profession (or developing within it), Shulman argues, requires knowledge, understanding, and faculties in problem-solving (the head) as well as the practical hands-on skills to perform specific tasks (the hand). It also involves the continual re-evaluation of beliefs, attitudes, and values, to develop the personal qualities (the heart) to act ethically and responsibly within a professional role. This suggests that models of coaching which focus on exploring dilemmas have a role to play alongside models such as instructional coaching, which are arguably more concerned with the 'hand' and the 'head.' For Shulman, acceptable professional practice, whatever the occupational sector, should not have any of the three core components (of the 'head,' 'heart,' and 'hand') missing.

A model for 'Dilemma-Based Coaching' for education was developed through a European-funded Erasmus strategic project called 'PROMISE' (Promoting Inclusion in Society through Education: Professional Dilemmas in Practice), which was led by Leeds Beckett University in England, and included partners from Germany, Hungary, the Netherlands, Slovenia and Scotland (Lofthouse, 2021). Using this model, coachees are supported to identify and articulate a dilemma that is either ongoing within their practice, or one that is starting to emerge. The role of the coach is to support coachees to have a reflective 'conversation-with-the-situation' underpinning this dilemma, through questions such as:

- Did you try anything new in relation to this dilemma?
- What are you learning about others and yourself as you engage more in this dilemma?
- Do you see things differently at all, and if so can you talk about that?
- What might be the legacy of this approach in your setting and practice?
- How might other educators gain insights from your experiences?

(Lofthouse, 2021)

Guidance on the use of 'Dilemma-Based Coaching' (DBC), created by a network of teachers and researchers associated with Leeds Beckett University and the Leeds Learning Alliance in England, is based on the experiences of educators, of working with it (Lofthouse, 2021). According to this guidance, meaningful DBC conversations tend to take between 20 and 30 minutes. To have sufficient value, according to this guidance, DBC tends to need to apply broader principles for high-quality coaching conversations, such as being coachee-led (Lofthouse, Leat and Towler, 2010) and distinct from conversations that take place as part of formal processes such as line management (Knight, Hock and Knight, 2016).

The approach of DBC, which was developed through the 'PROMISE' Project, is arguably distinct because it requires any dilemma being discussed to be made explicit, from the earliest stages of a coaching conversation. This enables educators who are familiar with the approach to mentally prepare for being coached in advance by considering possible dilemmas they might bring into the coaching conversation. Other models of coaching, however, may be more suitable in situations where the educator being coached is not consciously aware of what their dilemma is, and may benefit from talking through some of the stresses and strains they are encountering in their current practice, in order to identify it. In this scenario, questions from a coach, which support an exploration of the various choices a practitioner might have, and which aspects of a situation they do/do not hold responsibility over, may be preferable. However, although initial difficulties a teacher may experience, with identifying professional dilemmas, may be an obstacle to beginning to work with DBC, there are possible benefits to persisting through them. It is through such persistence that the articulation of professional dilemmas may develop into a habit for teachers, as they become more experienced with DBC. This, in turn, enables greater depth of interaction with the complexities and ambiguities underpinning their practice.

Approach Five: Philosophy for Teacher Education

Facilitation methods associated with the methodology of 'Philosophy for Children' (P4C) have been adapted and applied to teacher education. As was the case in sessions related to the research study on which this book is largely based, this can create the conditions through which groups of teachers can analyse dilemmas to collectively address broad questions around the ultimate aims and purpose of education.

The methodology of 'Philosophy for Children' (P4C) was developed for facilitating dialogue and enquiry (Lipman, 1976). A typical P4C session involves learners creating philosophical enquiry questions, reaching a decision on a question to discuss, and then engaging in a discussion on that question. In doing this, learners form and collectively build a 'Community of Enquiry' within their classroom, with a positive and inclusive culture that is conducive to learning. Although a high-profile randomised control trial on P4C in English schools found that its use did not lead to overall improvements in levels of reading, 96% of teachers in the intervention group, implementing the approach, reported that it led to greater respect for others amongst pupils and more confident expression (Education Endowment Foundation, 2021). Central to P4C are the '4Cs' of 'Critical Thinking,' 'Collaborative Thinking,'

'Caring Thinking,' and 'Creative Thinking.' Across the literature on P4C, these 4Cs are emphasised as an outcome of being part of a 'Community of Enquiry.'

The methodology of 'Philosophy for Teacher Education' (e.g., Orchard, Heilbronn and Winstanley, 2016) adopts very similar methods to P4C, to establish 'Communities of Enquiry' amongst educators, to facilitate their continued professional development. As an approach, it offers possibilities for enabling dilemma-based professional learning. This was evident, for example, in workshops which utilised methods associated with 'Philosophy for Teacher Education,' that were based on various 'dilemma stories' that underpinned the research study that is discussed within the chapters of this book.

Through my research and practice as a teacher educator, I have found that once anonymised (and generalised so not to enable individuals and schools to be identifiable) narratives of teachers' dilemmas can serve as allegorical exemplars to support 'Philosophy for Teacher Education.' Using narratives in this way has parallels with the 'Socratic Case Method' (SCM) that is central to the training of legal professionals. Through the SCM, various case histories are discussed, and debates take place around different possible interpretations of the law (and various principles enshrined in law) that could be made in relation to them. For legal training, the SCM is an example of what Shulman (2000) refers to as a 'signature pedagogy' (pp. 15–17).

Although the SCM tends not to be a 'signature pedagogy' for those training to teach (and neither for the continuing professional development of educators), Judith Shulman's writings can be applied to make a case for its use in teacher education. The point made by Lee Shulman that learning professional practice involves a simultaneous apprenticeship of the 'head,' 'heart,' and 'hand,' for example (i.e., that practitioners need to devote themselves to developing their knowledge, values, and skills) emphasises the multidimensional and interconnected nature of this. Whereas we might associate the development of 'the heart' with DBC, or the analysis of critical incidents, we can also use both of these to consider ways in which technical skills for teaching could improve. Although we might associate instructional coaching with the development of precise skills for teaching and the development of 'the hand,' it also offers scope for simultaneous dialogue around knowledge and professional values. Similarly, although the SCM of discussing particular situations and dilemmas tends to be a 'signature pedagogy' for legal training, there is likely also value in law students having extended work placements, as teachers do on an initial teacher training course, and for the SCM being adapted for the education of teachers.

An example of a 'Philosophy for Teacher Education' session was centred around the 'dilemma stories,' which my PhD research was based on, and which formed the basis for much of the discussion within this book. This session (or variations of it) have been delivered in multiple contexts, including with teachers on the MA Inclusive Practice in Education at Leeds Beckett University, practitioners engaging in school-based INSET (in-service education for teachers), a conference for educators at the Flanders Department for Education in Brussels, and workshops that took place in Latvia and Portugal, that were funded via the European commission Erasmus+ programme.

One activity within this session involved teachers working in small breakout groups to sort titles of a sample of the stories, which were presented to them in an envelope, on small cards. The template, which was used to create these cards, is shared in Table 10.3. As each story title was a question, which represented the dilemma within a story, they served as valuable stimuli for discussion, even without the full details of the story being given.

Table 10.3 Card sort activity to provoke discussion on the stories

Corridor Kids: Is there a better way?	How do I encourage Lenny to join in the RE lessons?
Is it possible to engage pupils of all abilities when teaching technology as a whole class?	How do we support Thomas to stay calm in the mainstream classroom?
How do we support Jack to have a good day in nursery?	How can I get all pupils to have input in my mixed-attainment secondary English Class?
Is Katie Being Under the Table an Issue?	How can I support Jane to be positive about teaching pupils with Profound and Multiple Learning Difficulties?
What is Stopping the Teachers I Work with from Using Assistive Technologies?	What does Inclusion Look Like for a Learner with Complex Medical Needs who is Self-Isolating?
Is it necessary for children to be creating Art in an Art lesson?	How can I get Ethan to feel positive about coming into school?
How can I strengthen inclusion within the current Year 6?	How can we support Claire to communicate?
How do we keep these boys in school?	Do I need to give Tyler a separate worksheet?
Should I really be accepting the argument 'all teachers are teachers of SEND' when we have a SEND department I don't find particularly helpful?	How do we ensure that the learning of our pupils with Severe Learning Difficulties is being fully supported in Key Stage Four Religious Education lessons?
Should I be having this conversation about death?	Is the provision for Annam in my tutor group good enough?
How will I manage my form group when Stephanie comes back to school and announces she now wants to be known as Steve?	Should I be insisting that my pupil with a diagnosis of Asperger's Syndrome attempt group work, even though she is reluctant to join in with it?
Should I have asked Chloe to take off the fairy wings?	Am I doing something right if those 'challenging pupils' are actually fine for me in my lesson?

When sorting the cards, each breakout group was asked to explore the following:

- Which dilemmas interest you?
- Which remind you of dilemmas you have experienced yourself?
- Do you have any advice or insight for the teacher(s) experiencing the dilemma?
- How might you sort the dilemmas into categories?

Each breakout group, therefore, could decide on any categories or reasons for grouping story titles together. Some groups, for example, chose to sort the groups into two piles; 'dilemmas that are familiar' and 'dilemmas that are unfamiliar.' Other groups decided to rank the cards according to the extent to which they felt confident enough to delve deeper into the dilemma and consider ways to respond to it.

In the session, the story titles effectively exemplified the notion of professional dilemmas, making it easier for participating teachers to identify dilemmas of their own, to share and discuss within the safe space that had been created. It also enabled the group to fully engage with a follow-up activity which involved the formulation of broader questions such as 'What is in Inclusive Teacher?' to provoke discussion.

Conclusion

Rather than use any of the approaches to dilemma-based professional learning, outlined within this chapter, in isolation, it is arguably possible for approaches to be combined and to work alongside one another. The approach of 'DBC,' for example, could potentially underpin the professional conversations that take place within a 'LS' or 'Learning Study.' In different 'Philosophy for Teacher Education' sessions, which were based on the teacher's 'dilemma stories,' the approach of DBC was adapted in a variety of ways, to enable teachers to benefit from Schon's 'reflection-on-action' and/or 'reflection-in-action' and/or identify critical incidents. In one workshop, for example, teachers were asked to take a few moments to silently identify a dilemma they had experienced, using the prompts on the PowerPoint slide depicted in Figure 10.5. They were then given 15 minutes to either draw or write about this dilemma, before getting into a breakout group with others, to share reflections, and consider any broad questions about professional values that may be starting to emerge.

In another session, teachers were asked to coach one another in pairs, using the framework outlined in Figure 10.6.

This particular workshop, therefore, was both a 'Philosophy for Teacher Education' session and training for teachers on the use of DBC. In the workshop, following the paired DBC conversations, teachers were asked to

130 Severe, Profound and Multiple Learning Difficulties in School

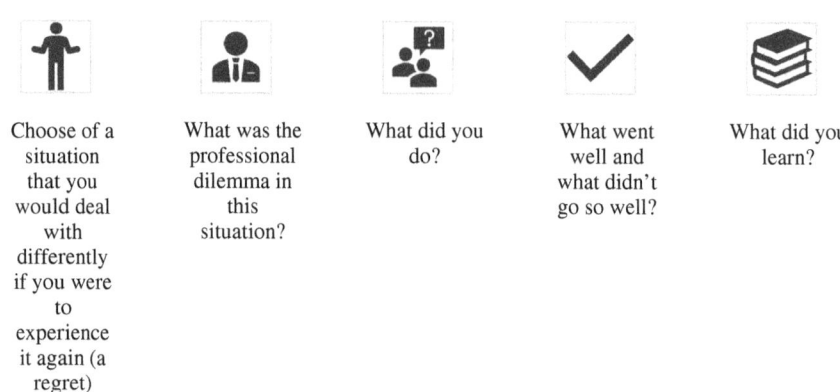

Figure 10.5 Prompts for facilitating dilemma-based dialogues between teachers.

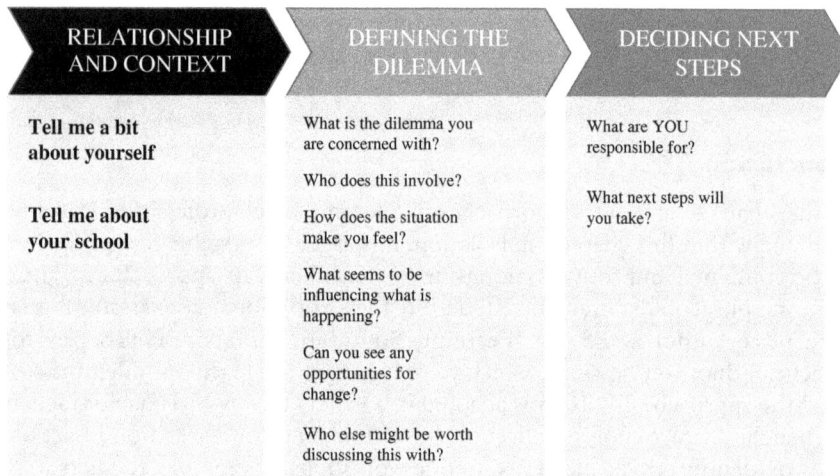

Figure 10.6 A process for micro dilemma-based coaching dialogues within a professional learning session.

return to breakout groups to sort the cards outlined in Figure 10.7, which outlines advice and/or good practice protocols for coaches, based on guidance developed by Leeds Beckett University and Leeds Learning Alliance (Lofthouse, 2021).

It could easily be argued that engaging in professional learning activities, based on 'Philosophy for Teacher Education', is by no means the most effective

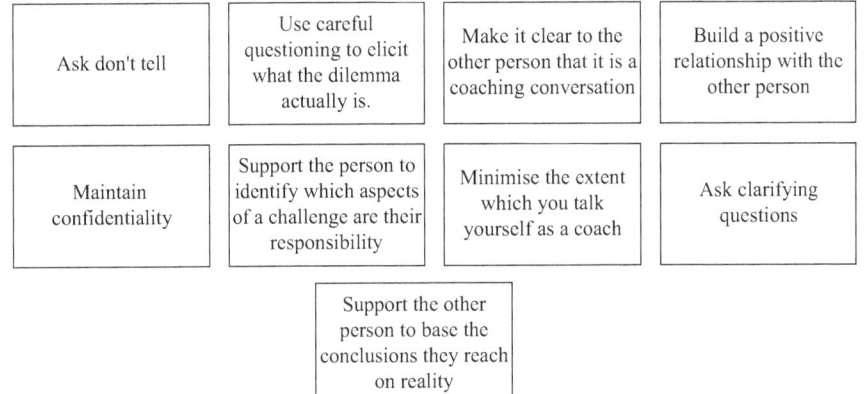

Figure 10.7 A card sort activity for use in a professional learning session, on dilemma-based coaching, through which participants arrange the various 'tips' for coaches.

use of a teacher's time. Within schools with learners with SPMLD, Philosophy for Teacher Education (or in any other dilemma-based approach to professional learning for that matter) could be seen as a selfish intellectual indulgence. It could be seen as something which prompts teachers to be inappropriately naval-gazing and esoteric, rather than focussed on the more mundane day-to-day realities around things such as peg feeding, or preventing self-harming behaviours, that teachers can only be prepared for through essential training, which may already be difficult to schedule and afford. However, whilst the impact of dilemma-based professional learning may not be immediate, easily measurable, or obvious, its absence from teacher education seemingly has harmful consequences. My experiences in schools, as well as the experiences of various colleagues and professional associates over the years, demonstrate this. When classroom practice becomes merely about knowledge and skills (the 'head' and the 'hand'), they become dogma, and practitioner attention shifts towards fidelity to these knowledge and skills, rather than on the learners themselves. In relation to this, I would like to ask you to imagine a 15-year-old learner, with the label 'PMLD' who may be described by some professionals as 'ambulant', so could walk. This learner is pre-verbal, doubly incontinent, and does not seem to have the awareness and coordination, to feed themselves. They also do not respond to their own name, whenever it is called, and rarely demonstrate indicators of engagement, such as 'anticipation', when a routine experience, such as singing a song, is repeated for them. I would also like to ask you to imagine how, this same learner can be seen, strapped into a specialist chair, in several videos that have been uploaded to the assessment and reporting App which her school uses (which would have most likely taken considerable force). In one of these videos, she is having her arms and hands manipulated by a teaching assistant, so that she appears to be pointing at the correct shape on the tray in front of her, whenever its name is called out. In another video, she seems to be asleep, whilst being read a book from the phonics reading scheme which teachers have attended a course on. You are surprised that the school feels no shame in showing you these videos, and in sharing them with the learner's family. In fact, staff at the school are proud of the videos and seem to view what is going on in them as high-quality teaching. This seems to be because it emulates what is seen to be high-quality teaching with different learners, in different contexts. In this scenario, without Schon's 'reflection-in-action' and/or 'reflection-on-action,' there seems to be little (if any) consideration of how the same action within a classroom may be simultaneously inclusive and exclusive, and of how practice that may be beneficial and enabling in some classroom situations may actually cause harm and distress in others. This book is dedicated to all the learners who have had to endure approaches such as those experienced by this unnamed learner, who, in my own experience, is representative of so many. This book is also dedicated to the very many education professionals who have worked hard to resist such approaches and ensure that 'the heart' of pedagogical practice remains in classrooms.

References

Black-Hawkins, K., & Florian, L. (2012). Classroom teachers craft knowledge of their inclusive practice. *Teachers and Teaching: Theory and Practice*, *18*(5). https://doi.org/10.1080/13540602.2012.709732

Carpenter, B., Brooks, T., Cockbill, B., Fotheringham, J., & Rawson, H. (2011). *Complex Learning Difficulties and Disabilities Research Project: Final Report*. Retrieved from http://complexneeds.org.uk/modules/Module-3.2-Engaging-in-learning---key-approaches/All/downloads/m10p010d/the_complex_learning_difficulties.pdf

Davies, G. (2025, 10th May). *Attention Autism*. Retrieved from https://ginadavies.co.uk/attention-autism/

Dolaty, S., Tait, N., & Brunskill, H. (2022). *Youth Participation: Models Used to Understand Young People's Participation in School and Community Programmes*. London, England: UCL/Anna Freud Centre.

Dudley, P. (2014a). Lesson Study: Professional learning for our time. In *Lesson Study: Professional Learning for Our Time*. London: Routledge. https://doi.org/10.4324/9780203795538

Dudley, P. (2014b). *Lesson Study: A Handbook*. Retrieved from: https://lessonstudy.co.uk/lesson-study-a-handbook/

Dudley, P., Xu, H., Vermunt, J. D., & Lang, J. (2019). Empirical evidence of the impact of lesson study on students' achievement, teachers' professional learning and on institutional and system evolution. *European Journal of Education*, *54*(2). https://doi.org/10.1111/ejed.12337

Education Endowment Foundation. (2021, November). *Philosophy for Children: Second Trial*. Retrieved from http://educationendowmentfoundation.org.uk/projects-and-evaluation/projects/philosophy-for-children-effectiveness-trial

Edwards, T. (2021). Developing the methodology of Lesson Study to enhance the spiritual, moral, social and cultural development of pupils with moderate learning difficulties in a UK special school setting. In S. L. Goei, B. Norwich, & P. Dudley (Eds.), *Lesson Study in Inclusive Educational Settings* (1st ed., pp. 121–137). Routledge. https://doi.org/10.4324/9781315668581-6-6

Elliott, J. (2009). *Lesson and Learning Study: a globalizing form of teacher research.* Retrieved from https://www.eduhk.hk/wals/website/resources/Lesson_and_Learning_Study.pdf

Florian, L. (2010). The concept of inclusive pedagogy. In *Transforming the Role of the SENCO: Achieving the National Award for SEN Coordination* (Vol. 1, pp. 62–70). Maidenhead, England: Open University Press.

Florian, L., & Beaton, M. (2018). Inclusive pedagogy in action: Getting it right for every child. *International Journal of Inclusive Education, 22*(8). https://doi.org/10.1080/13603116.2017.1412513

Forster, S. (2010). Age-appropriateness: Enabler or barrier to a good life for people with profound intellectual and multiple disabilities? *Journal of Intellectual and Developmental Disability, 35*(2). https://doi.org/10.3109/13668251003694606

Hagger, H., & McIntyre, D. (2006). *Learning Teaching from Teachers: Realising the Potential of School-Based Teacher Education.* Maidenhead, England: Open University Press.

Hart, R. (1992). Children's Participation: From Tokenism to citizenship. In *Unicef: Innocenti Essays* (Vol. 4). Florence, Italy: UNICEF International Child Development Centre.

Innabi, H., & Emanuelsson, J. (2021). Enrichment in school principals' ways of seeing mathematics. *International Journal of Mathematical Education in Science and Technology, 52*(10). https://doi.org/10.1080/0020739X.2020.1782496

Knight, J. (2007). *Instructional Coaching: A Partnership Approach to Improving Instruction.* California: Corwin Press.

Knight, D. S., Hock, M., & Knight, J. (2016). Designing instructional coaching. In *Instructional-Design Theories and Models: The Learner-Centered Paradigm of Education* (Vol. 4). https://doi.org/10.4324/9781315795478

Lipman, M. (1976). Philosophy for children. *Metaphilosophy,* 17–39.

Ling Lo, M. (2012). *Variation Theory and the Improvement of Teaching and Learning.* Gothenburg: Gothenburg University Press.

Lofthouse, R. (2021, 20 April). *Exploring and learning from educational complexity through dilemma-based coaching.* Retrieved from https://www.leedsbeckett.ac.uk/blogs/carnegie-education/2021/04/exploring-and-learning-from-educational-complexity/

Orchard, J., Heilbronn, R., & Winstanley, C. (2016). Philosophy for Teachers (P4T): Developing new teachers' applied ethical decision-making. *Ethics and Education, 11*(1), 42–54. https://doi.org/10.1080/17449642.2016.1145495

Lofthouse, R. M., Leat, D., & Towler, C. (2010). *Improving Teacher Coaching in Schools: A Practical Guide (Project report).* National College for Teaching and Leadership.

Magnusson, J., Kullberg, A., Innabi, H., Knutsson, L., von Otter, A. M., & Landström, J. (2021). Prospective teachers' opportunities to develop PCK from participation in learning study. *Educational Action Research.* https://doi.org/10.1080/09650792.2021.1997779

Marton, F. (1981). Phenomenography: Describing conceptions of the world around us. *Instructional Science, 10*(2). https://doi.org/10.1007/BF00132516

Norwich, B., (2014) *Lesson Study for Assessment: Introduction and Guidelines.* Exeter: University of Exeter Graduate School of Education. Retrieved from https://www.lessonstudysend.co.uk

Norwich, B. (2010). Dilemmas of difference, curriculum and disability: International perspectives. *Comparative Education*, *46*(2). https://doi.org/10.1080/03050061003775330

Norwich, B., Benham-Clarke, S., & Goei, S. L. (2021). Review of research literature about the use of lesson study and lesson study-related practices relevant to the field of special needs and inclusive education. *European Journal of Special Needs Education*, *36*(3). https://doi.org/10.1080/08856257.2020.1755929

Norwich, B., Koutsouris, G., Fujita, T., Ralph, T., Adlam, A., & Milton, F. (2016). Exploring knowledge bridging and translation in lesson study using an inter-professional team. *International Journal for Lesson and Learning Studies*, *5*(3). https://doi.org/10.1108/IJLLS-02-2016-0006

Pask, R., & Joy, B. (2007). *Mentoring-Coaching: A Guide for Education Professionals*. Maidenhead, England: Open University Press.

Paulsrud, D. (2024). Resolving dilemmas: Swedish special educators and subject teachers' perspectives on their enactment of inclusive education. *Journal of Education Policy*, *39*(2). https://doi.org/10.1080/02680939.2023.2210102

Schon, D. A. (1991). *The Reflective Practitioner: How Professionals Think in Action*. Avebury: Basic Books.

Shulman, J. H. (2000). Case methods as a bridge between standards and classroom practice. *National Partnership for Excellence and Accountability in Teaching*. Retrieved from https://files.eric.ed.gov/fulltext/ED452188.pdf

Shulman, L. (2007, 21 October). The Many Faces of Engagement. *13th Annual Conference of the Coalition of Urban and Metropolitan Universities*. Retrieved from https://journals.indianapolis.iu.edu/index.php/muj/article/view/20330/19939

Standards and Testing Agency. (2024, 15 April). *Guidance: The engagement model*. Retrieved from https://www.gov.uk/government/publications/the-engagement-model/the-engagement-model

Treseder, P. (1997). *Empowering Children and Young People - Training Manual: Promoting Involvement in Decision-Making*. London, England: Save the Children.

Tripp, D. (2012). *Critical Incidents in Teaching: Developing Professional Judgement (Classical Edition)*. London: Routledge.

Welsh Government (2025). *Routes for Learning*. https://hwb.gov.wales/curriculum-for-wales/routes-for-learning

Index

Pages in *italics* refer to figures and pages in **bold** refer to tables.

ableism 3
active professionalism 75–76
Activist Professionalism 87, 90, 94–97
age appropriateness 16–17, 22, 95–96, 123
Applied Behavioural Analysis (ABA) 47, 72
Aristotle 26; Aristotelian phronesis 31–32; Aristotelian Virtue Ethics 30–31
art teaching 85–90
autism 3, 47–48, 70–76, 86–88
authenticity 55

Bentham, Jeremy 25, 28
Bryan, Jonathan 3, 40, 54

Capabilities Approach 28–30; of Amartya Sen 29; of Martha Nussbaum 29–30
Care Ethics 36–37
Craft knowledge 31, 66, 73–74, 114–115, 121
collaboration 76, 106–109
consequentialism 26–28, 32, 65
critical incident analysis 123
curriculum 30, 37, 40–45, 53–55, 80, 89, 92–94

death 19, 61–68
'Degrees of Participation' model 121, **122**
dilemma-based coaching 123–126
dilemma of difference 17–19, 80–81
dilemmas of 'looking' 21, 81–82, 84, 96–97

dilemma of 'possibility' 19, 68
Dilemma of 'What Matters?' 21–22, 87–88, 95
Dilemma of 'What's Working?' 20, 71–75
Difference Principle 35
duty ethics 32–34

Engagement Model 103–105, 117–119, **118**

form tutoring 76–85
Four Dilemmas for Inclusive Practice *102*

Hart's Ladder of Participation 121, **122**

identity-first language 74–75
inclusion 9–14, 102
Inclusive Pedagogy 11, 49–51, 54, 66–67, 83
Inclusive Pedagogical Approach in Action framework 68
Independent Living Movement 14
individualism 109
inherited conventions of schooling 85–86
instructional coaching 123
intersectionality 12

Kant, Immanuel 32–35

Learning Study 119–123
Lesson Study 115–119; definition 115; cycle 117
lifeskills 82

Managerial Professionalism 76
meritocracy 36
Mill, J.S 25–26

Noddings, Nel 36–37; expressed and inferred Needs 36, 66–67
Nussbaum, Martha 15, 29–30; Ten Central Capabilities 29, 65, 88

pedagogy 45–46
person-first language 74–75
phenomenological research 18, 102–103
Philosophy for teacher education 126–129
phronesis 31
postcolonial theory 13
Profound and Multiple Learning Difficulties: definition 1–2; prevalence 3; provision 91–97
promoting independence 14–16

Randomised Control Trials (RCTs) 20, 71–75
Rawls, John 35–36; Difference Principle 35; Veil of Ignorance 35
Religious Education 61–68
Routes for Learning 119

Schon, D 124
Salamanca Statement 10
Sen, Amartya 29
SEND Code of Practice 14–15
Severe Learning Difficulties: definitions 1–2, 78–84
Social Model of Disability 14
Socratic Case Method 127
special schools debate 79
Spivak, Gayatri 13
staff wellbeing 105–106

task analysis 88–90
teacher agency 20, 55, 103–105
teacher education 51–53, 114
teleological ethics 26–28
Ten Central Capabilities 29, 65–66
Topographical Pedagogy 109–113, **110**

utilitarianism 25–28, 32, 64–65, 72, 75

virtue ethics 30–31
Vygotsky, Lev 50–51

Warnock Report 18, 81

For Product Safety Concerns and Information please contact our EU
representative GPSR@taylorandfrancis.com
Taylor & Francis Verlag GmbH, Kaufingerstraße 24, 80331 München, Germany

www.ingramcontent.com/pod-product-compliance
Lightning Source LLC
Chambersburg PA
CBHW070310230426
43664CB00015B/2703